NICK HOLDSTOCK is a journalist and writer whose work has appeared in the *London Review of Books*, the *Times Literary Supplement* and the *Guardian*. He is the author of two books about Xinjiang, *The Tree That Bleeds* (2011) and *China's Forgotten People: Xinjiang, Terror and the Chinese State* (I.B.Tauris, 2015). His first novel, *The Casualties*, was published in 2015. He lives in Edinburgh.

'At last, a book about China that takes the long view, showing how the "Chinese Dream" is playing out for a fascinating cast of characters that author Nick Holdstock has known for years. He writes with great warmth and deep empathy, capturing the realities of everyday life in places that foreign and Chinese correspondents pass by. I couldn't put it down.'

MICHAEL MEYER, author of
In Manchuria and *The Last Days of Old Beijing*

CHASING
THE
CHINESE
DREAM

STORIES FROM MODERN CHINA

NICK HOLDSTOCK

I.B. TAURIS
LONDON · NEW YORK

First published in 2017 by
I.B.Tauris & Co. Ltd
London · New York
www.ibtauris.com

ISBN: 978 1 78453 373 1
eISBN: 978 1 78672 220 1
ePDF: 978 1 78673 220 0

A full CIP record for this book is available from the British Library
A full CIP record is available from the Library of Congress

Library of Congress Catalog Card Number: available

Text designed and typeset by Tetragon, London
Printed and bound in Sweden by ScandBook AB

CONTENTS

PROVINCES AND REGIONS IN THE
PEOPLE'S REPUBLIC OF CHINA

HUNAN PROVINCE

AUTHOR'S NOTE

Some of the names of my interviewees have been changed, either at their own request, or because it seemed prudent. At the time of writing, one US dollar was equivalent to 6.5 yuan.

The research that forms part of this book first appeared in the *Dublin Review*, the *Los Angeles Review of Books*, the *Guardian* and on the *London Review of Books* blog.

BIG CITY DREAMS

For two years I taught English in a small city famous for clementines and murder. The clementines' reputation was well deserved: they were at their sour best when green-skinned. As for the murders, if any took place, they were very discreet.

Shaoyang is an old city in the southern province of Hunan. It spreads along the junction of two rivers: the pale jade Shao River and the wider, brown Zi River. When I arrived in 1999 the city's population was just under half a million. From the city gate I could look over an expanse of old houses whose roofs of thick grey tiles overlapped like scales. In some respects the city hadn't changed much from the description offered by Dr George Pearson, a Christian missionary who lived in Shaoyang from 1920 to 1950:

> Back then it was still a sleepy old place, with its stone wall built long before Christ. Every night its gates were shut to keep out bandits. Its streets were dark and very narrow with no room for cars or carts; there were stone steps everywhere, up and down. All traffic had to come and go carried by men. Passengers were carried in sedan chairs; all the shops were open to the street; there were no glass fronts.[1]

Fifty years later the old city wall had gone, but at night many streets were still unlit. Most of the shops were in garage-like units that had roll-down shutters instead of doors. On the pavements people washed vegetables in plastic bowls, impaled eels on nails, and welded engine blocks. And everywhere the old stone steps still went up and down.

The teacher training college where I worked was on the edge of town. Behind the student dormitories there were just rice fields. English seemed to be regarded as a girls' subject – 90 per cent of my students were female. They were between 18 and 21, but seemed far younger. Their pencil cases and bags were covered with stickers of baby rabbits and kittens. They loved to sing songs. Any mention of boyfriends or kissing made them giggle and blush. When I asked my students what their parents did for a living, most said, 'My mother is a peasant,' or, 'My father is a farmer.'

At times the college felt like a cross between a prison camp and an orphanage. Students were fined if they missed the 6 a.m. morning exercise drill or were late to class. Much of their free time was spent listening to political speeches or picking up litter around campus. Their only possible response to this situation was to say *mei ban fa*, which means 'there's no choice'. It's a phrase of resignation.

Most students were only at Shaoyang Teachers' College because their scores on the *gaokao*, the National Higher Education Entrance Examination, were too low for them to get into a good university. Few of them wanted to be high-school teachers, because the pay was low and working conditions were poor: in the countryside, middle-school classes often had over 50 students, and there were few facilities except a blackboard and basic textbooks. The few students who expressed an interest in teaching usually explained their decision with platitudes like 'Teaching is the most glorious job under the sun.' In more candid moments they spoke of pressure from their parents, who viewed teaching as a steady job.

On a wet day in February 2000, I was returning to Shaoyang after visiting friends in a nearby town for Chinese New Year. From the train window I looked out onto a landscape dissolved by rain. The fields were flooded, the hills a blur; no one was in sight. We passed clusters of houses built of faded brick whose doorways were framed by bright strips of red paper on which golden characters asked for luck, good health and double happiness.

As soon as the train pulled into Shaoyang it was clear something was wrong. Police officers stood in a long line on the platform. Behind them was a crowd of around five hundred people. As I got off the train the crowd began to shout and push. Then the police line dissolved and the crowd surged forward. All I could do was stand with my back to a pillar as people rushed to get on the train. The crush was worst around the train doors; some avoided this by climbing up the side of the carriage and clambering through the windows. One small man threw his sack in, then found he was too short to climb up. He had to be pulled up by two men inside, both of whom looked delighted to add another person to a carriage that was already full.

Whistles were blown as more people climbed through the windows. The platform was a mass of people pushing and shouting while dragging sacks and bags and boxes. I got out my camera and was able to take three or four pictures before a policeman shouted at me. I pretended not to hear, and turned and walked away. He caught up with me, pointed to the camera, and said, 'Give me that.' I didn't argue. For the next ten seconds I had the petty pleasure of watching him struggle to find the lever that opened the back of the camera. Then, with a triumphant pop, the film was exposed.

The train was headed south; its passengers were migrant workers who had been visiting their home towns at Chinese New Year (also known as Spring Festival). They were going back to jobs in Guangzhou, Shenzhen, Dongguan and other cities in southern Guangdong province. Similar scenes were taking place in stations all over the country. People were saying goodbye to relatives, spouses and children, then cramming themselves onto trains and buses. In 2000 there were 85 million migrant workers in China; in 2014 this figure had increased to 275 million.

In some respects, China's holiday-season travel boom is analogous to the Christmas or Thanksgiving travel rush in the West. But the ways in which it differs from this are instructive. The most obvious is the scale of the migration. Before the 2014 Spring Festival travel period it was estimated that around 3.6 billion passenger trips would be taken, most of them on public transport. Whilst there's no exact figure for the number of people travelling during the period, it could be as many as 800–900 million, around three-quarters of the population. Given the staggering numbers of people on the move, it's unsurprising that travel during this period has its own proper noun: *Chunyun*.

The railways are the most popular method of transport during *Chunyun*, since many can't afford plane tickets. To say, as a general manager at China Railway did in 2013, 'There is a big gap between railway transportation capacity and demand'[2] is something of an understatement. Buying train tickets for long-distance travel in China often isn't a simple matter, even during normal travel periods – tickets for sleeper berths sell out quickly, and are sometimes not available without paying a ticket scalper or knowing someone who works for the railways. The ability to buy tickets online has made things less chaotic: before this people would often queue for days, only to find that all the tickets were gone within minutes of going on sale.

The intense competition for tickets has led to fights, near-riots and acts of desperation. In January 2011, a man in Jinhua city, in Zhejiang province, ran clad in just a pair of tight boxer briefs through the ticket hall after being told there were no more tickets for his train. After being made to put on his clothes, he went to the station manager's office and stripped again.[3]

For those lucky enough to get a ticket, there is often the prospect of having to stand for more than a day. And this isn't standing in the sense that most people in the US and Europe are used to. If you can picture a situation where it may not even be possible to put both feet on the *floor*, then you may approach the condition of the trains during *Chunyun*. As for the consequences of so many people having to share a small number of toilets over such a long period, I leave that to your imagination.

Unsurprisingly, people have been known to collapse from fatigue or dehydration. Theft is not uncommon – some insurance companies have policies that specifically cover travel during *Chunyun*. Given the perils and discomfort of public transport during *Chunyun*, some travellers have sought alternatives. On a number of occasions people have walked hundreds of miles to get back to their home towns, but travelling by motorbike has become a more popular option. In 2013 more than 100,000 migrant workers went home from Guangdong this way, despite the fact that some would be travelling for days, often on poor roads through mountainous terrain.

The reason why these huge numbers of workers need to travel so far is in many ways the story of China's remarkable economic boom over the last three decades. This has been mainly due to its manufacturing sector, which makes most of the computers we use, the TVs we watch, the clothes we wear, the light bulbs in our houses. In the late 1970s there was a radical shift in the economic vision of China's leaders, which led to the 'opening up' of the country to foreign investors, initially with the designation of Shenzhen, then a small town of 300,000, as a Special Economic Zone. The abundance of cheap labour, much of it from the countryside, made China an attractive place for multinationals to open factories. Shenzhen was selected mainly for its proximity to Hong Kong, rather than any pre-existing industry; in 1979 it was all rice fields. Now Shenzhen's population is over 10 million, and still growing.

In most countries it's common for people to travel to larger cities in order to find work. But whereas people who move to London, Rio or Bangkok for work often end up staying there, perhaps buying a home, this isn't an option for most migrant workers in China. Every Chinese citizen has a *hukou*, a document that ties them to a specific place, initially where one of their parents is registered as living (it used to be only the mother, but now either parent's residence can be used). A person's ability to claim rights to basic services such as health and education is limited to the area in which they are registered, and the same applies to their children.

The *hukou* system grew out of a method of family registration in ancient China that was used to impose taxation and conscription. The modern *hukou* system dates from 1958, and like many other political and bureaucratic aspects of Communist China has its roots in the Soviet Union (where the system was known as *propiska*). The aim of the *hukou* system was to ensure there would be enough agricultural workers to supply the industry-oriented cities with food. At that time, the system was especially restrictive. A farmer wanting to visit the city would need a letter from his or her local authority just to buy a train ticket or stay in a hotel. During the Great Famine of 1958–62, when around 36 million people starved to death, whether one had a rural or urban *hukou* was often a matter of life or death: city dwellers were guaranteed a daily calorie allowance as they were deemed more important for China's development.

For the next 20 years, people from the countryside were mostly kept out of major cities unless their labour was temporarily needed in the factories. It wasn't until the agricultural collectives were dismantled in the early 1980s that people were allowed to come and work in the cities. But the *hukou* system was, and is, a system of apartheid. Rural migrants are second-class city-dwellers. Without a local urban *hukou* a person can't get subsidised public housing, education for their children, healthcare, a pension or unemployment benefits, no matter how long they've been living in that city. The *hukou* system is the main reason people have to travel so far to find work, and why so many people's lives end up being split between where they work and where most of their family live.

Back in 2000, I didn't connect the migrant workers in that chaotic train station with my students in the college, even though I knew that the majority of them, despite being trained as teachers, wanted to find other jobs. Most said they wanted to go into business, be a manager or work as a translator for a foreign company. Most thought their English was too valuable an asset to be wasted on teaching. Some spoke of 'jumping the dragon gate' (*Liyu Tiao Long Men*), a saying that refers to an old story of how a carp can be transformed into a dragon if it swims to the top of a waterfall. This was originally used to refer to success in the imperial civil service exams, but nowadays is a metaphor for courage and perseverance against great odds.

For many years, their ambition would have been irrelevant. Graduates of the college were assigned jobs in schools by the government, and even after China's 'reform and opening up' process began in 1978, many still took the jobs allocated to them. But by the mid-1990s, everyone knew someone (or *of* someone) who had travelled to the south coast and found work and come back with more money than anyone could earn farming or teaching. What my students wanted was to be on those crowded trains going south.

After three decades of migration, the mass movement of workers seemed an immutable part of Chinese life. But in 2011 China's leaders announced plans that promised to radically alter this pattern. Like the Soviet Union, China outlines its social and economic goals in Five-Year Plans. In the 12th Five-Year Plan for 2011–15 they set the goal of having 70 per cent of the population living in cities by 2025. The plan envisaged 250 million people leaving the countryside and becoming registered city dwellers – what was called the 'greatest planned migration in human history'.[4] Though the plan offered few specifics (*hukou* reform has been part of previous Five-Year Plans, with little consequence) the only way for these people to become permanent city dwellers is for them to be allowed to shift their *hukou* to the city, or for the *hukou* system to be abolished.

This isn't an entirely new trend, more the culmination of one. China's leaders have been promoting urbanisation for the last three decades. During the 1980s, the urban population grew by

110 million; in the 1990s an additional 157 million become urban residents; and during the first decade of the twenty-first century an extra 210 million were living in China's cities. Nationwide, the current urban population of 670 million (almost double the population of the US) is more than three times what it was in 1980. In 2011 China became a predominantly urban country.

The new phase of urbanisation aims to boost China's economy. Though China's economy has grown remarkably since the 1980s, in recent years its growth has slowed. This is partly because China's ability to offer cheap labour to make goods for export is diminishing as wages and living standards continue to rise. The 12th Five-Year Plan was thus a blueprint for a different kind of economy – and by implication, a different society. It envisaged a China where the majority of people live in cities and do what every economy needs its citizens to do: buy stuff. According to Li Keqiang, the Chinese premier, 'urbanization has the greatest potential for boosting domestic demand.'[5]

While the above might make good economic sense, it isn't exactly inspiring. The Chinese government put a more idealistic spin on the plan by stressing that urbanisation was a crucial part of the 'Chinese Dream'. This concept was first introduced in a speech in 2012 by the Chinese president, Xi Jinping. The following year it was popularised by a poster campaign that stressed a number of personal and national ideals like patriotism, thrift and the importance of family. According to Xi, the aim of the Chinese Dream was to improve people's livelihoods and prosperity, construct a better society and strengthen the military.[6] While these might sound like the typical goals of many developing nations, Xi also stressed that the Chinese Dream is a question of 'national rejuvenation'. The implication was that China isn't rising from nothing – it is returning to a former greatness.

The Chinese Dream may be an inspiring vision of prosperity for individuals and the nation, but it's also incredibly vague. Is everyone supposed to be dreaming the same dream? Is a man selling noodles on a street corner able to aspire to the same things as a woman driving past in her BMW? Is it really the dream of farmers to leave land their ancestors worked for generations? But for all its vagueness, the notion of the Chinese Dream does capture the sense of aspiration that has characterised Chinese society since the late 1970s – a period that Evan Osnos, the former *New Yorker* correspondent for China, aptly characterises as an 'age of ambition'. One of the most well-known posters for the Chinese Dream campaign features a clay figurine of a red-smocked peasant girl with a wistful expression.[7] The image was chosen because an official in the Propaganda Department felt that 'it represented longing and hope'.[8]

Given that Premier Li Keqiang has stressed that the government will be implementing 'a new type of people-centred urbanization',[9] it seems appropriate to explore how the transformation of its towns and cities is affecting people all over the country. The first part of this book looks at how some of my former students and colleagues from Shaoyang have fared in their attempts to find wealth and happiness – and sometimes reinvent themselves – in places far from Hunan.

The second part explores how the push to increase the number of people living in cities is reshaping Chinese society, and how people are trying to adapt to these profound changes. The growth of China's cities will have consequences for all of us, not least in environmental terms – some studies suggest that the carbon footprint of people living in cities is lower than that of people in the countryside (assuming the city is well designed and well governed).[10] Considering that China is the world's largest emitter of greenhouse gases, this would obviously be a good thing.

Though this book is set in many different places in China, in both villages and its biggest cities, I make no claim that it provides a portrait of the whole country, let alone its people. I've never been comfortable with top-down analyses of China, mainly because the country is so diverse: too much gets left out in the attempt to make some general pronouncement that ends up describing nothing recognisable. I prefer instead to focus on particular places and people. Most of the people I write about have some link to Hunan province, the place where in a very real sense China began for me. This is partly because I have a great affection for the place – the red clay of its soil, the hotness of its cooking, the lushness of the rice fields. It's also because Hunan, like many of China's central provinces, tends to be overlooked when people write about China, despite it being almost the size of the United Kingdom and home to 67 million people. These places are as much a part of the story of China's latest transformation as prosperous eastern cities like Beijing and Shanghai.

The 'Chinese Dream', as the Chinese government articulates it, may be about building national pride and prosperity, but then again it may just be a catchy slogan that aims to unite a whole set of policy initiatives that don't really belong together. What's certain is that China's leaders are once again profoundly altering the social and economic conditions of over a billion people's lives. In most respects, these people have no say over what happens to their village, town or city. But if there was one thing that many of the people I met had in common, it was that they were trying to adapt their goals (if you like, their Dreams) to a rapidly changing society. Most were constrained by a lack of money or connections, or by the unfavourable conditions created by China's *hukou* system. Yet, despite these obstacles, most had ways of coping with these barriers, at least potentially. They moved from the countryside to the city, and sometimes vice versa, changing jobs and neighbourhoods in their search for prosperity. They refused to say *mei ban fa*.

PART I

1

JUMPING THE DRAGON GATE

After I left Shaoyang I tried to stay in touch with many of my students. Over the next eight years I was only able to keep in direct contact with a small number of them, but through them I learned what had become of many of their classmates. Though most had entertained grand dreams of leaving both Shaoyang and Hunan province far behind, few had been successful. The majority were only able to find work in towns and cities within the province, and usually only as teachers. But for many of them this still constituted upward social mobility. These sons and daughters of farmers had become urban professionals.

In April 2010 I went back to China to visit two former students whose fortunes after graduation had differed greatly. Wenli was living in Shanghai, while Xiao Long was teaching in a school in the Hunan countryside. Both had been excellent students. Xiao Long's spoken English had been excellent, while Wenli had been one of the brightest, most politically savvy students, who spent his free time preparing for a succession of gala performances that commemorated key moments in the history of Chinese Communism. I wanted to know how such gifted carp had ended up at opposite ends of the waterfall.

*

I met Wenli on the platform of Shanghai's Dongchang underground station. He was wearing a grey T-shirt under a brown leather jacket with padded shoulders. On the T-shirt a woman's face was drawn in a pop-art style, her mouth open in either a gasp or a scream. His trousers were cream-coloured and tight without being skinny, and ended in a pair of worn Converse trainers. In other words, Wenli looked cool.

'You made it!' he said, and smiled, and the sight of his teeth – their discoloration and uneven spacing, the gums that appeared recessed – immediately recalled the young man who ten years earlier had gasped in wonder at photos of Hyde Park, who sometimes came to class with mud on his clothes from helping his relatives in the fields. But there was no time to reminisce. Already we were moving quickly down tunnels lined with pictures of futuristic buildings. One looked like a dead rabbit; another was just an explosion of spikes.

'These are Expo buildings,' said Wenli. 'It is a fair for world architecture. Many countries will have buildings there.'

'Will you go?'

'Yes; I am very interested in architecture. In China, we have too many ugly old buildings. We must make them modern.'

Outside it was a warm afternoon and the buildings seemed modern enough. For two or three blocks they were high and impersonal, their windows reflecting the clouds. We were in the Pudong district, on the east bank of Shanghai's Huangpu River, a district that in the late 1980s had still mostly been farmland and warehouses. After the fast growth of the Special Economic Zones in Shenzhen and Guangzhou, there were fears that Shanghai might be left behind. To remedy this a new central business district was planned for the area, one that would be China's equivalent of Manhattan. A torrent of official propaganda followed; in 1990 Deng Xiaoping, then Chinese premier, boasted that 'Shanghai is our trump card.'[1] But despite this enthusiasm, few wanted to relocate from the historic centre on the other bank of the Huangpu. By the start of the 2000s, this new area was only 30 per cent occupied. Outside China there was talk of the 'Shanghai Bubble', and doubts about China's economic health. The economist Milton Friedman articulated the general scepticism about Pudong in 2001 when he dubbed it 'a statist monument for a dead pharaoh on the level of the pyramids'.[2] The mayor of Shanghai defended the empty offices and apartment blocks by saying that the construction was 'like buying a suit a few sizes too big for a growing boy'.[3]

Since China 'opened up', it's been the target of gloomy predictions about its economic and political future – the imminent demise of its ruling Communist Party is regularly foretold. Often these messages of doom issue from pundits and commentators who fail to take into account the ways in which China's economic and political system differs from other countries. In the case of Pudong, one difference was that China's major banks are state-owned, so they could be forced to relocate. Fifteen years after Friedman's verdict, Pudong's occupancy rate is now comparable to Manhattan's. In many ways, Pudong has been a model of development for many municipalities, even those without its many advantages, which included a good location, a firm industrial base and existing prosperity in the region.

There seems to be no limit to the confidence of Shanghai's urban planners: at the time of writing the city is building another new area. Nanhui New City, located 60 kilometres south-east of the centre, is being built to provide accommodation, shops and services for a planned 800,000 residents. Construction is due to finish by 2020; the finished development will consist of concentric ring roads encircling a man-made lake, a design apparently inspired by 'the image of a drop falling into the water', according to the manager of the project.[4]

When I asked Wenli what he was doing in Shanghai, I expected him to say he worked as a translator or in the media.

'What am I doing?' he repeated, as if the question baffled him. 'I am a teacher; no, not a teacher. A trainer. I train students for the IELTS [International English Language Testing System] exam.'

'Do you like the job?'

'To be frank, I do not. I am not a real teacher. Just help them pass some test.'

'What about the students?'

'Some are arseholes, some are lazy, some are stupid.'

'So why do you do it?'

'For the money,' he said, and smiled in a way that was either rueful or proud.

We turned off onto a small street where two teenage girls in identical blue tracksuits were hitting a shuttlecock back and forth, watched by a third girl who was texting while eating sugar cane. We passed a hairdresser and a small supermarket, then Wenli asked me to wait. He disappeared into a small shop whose window was full of photos of afflicted skin. Boils, rashes, nodules, spots, blotches, welts and what appeared to be some sort of orange mollusc growing from a neck. As I stood there, wondering what else to ask Wenli, I remembered two things about him. The first was that his sister had killed herself after years of emotional problems. The second was that his final dissertation – a brilliant analysis of how corporations choose their names – had been almost entirely plagiarised.

Wenli came out holding a red plastic bag. He took me to a small restaurant below street level whose walls were covered with posters of waterfalls, flower-filled meadows and blonde women astride Harley-Davidsons, holding electric guitars. Our waitress was a short young woman with a fringe you could have used as a ruler. She asked us to pay in advance.

'How come?' I asked Wenli, because in Shaoyang (and most other cities in China) one usually pays after eating.

'It is because this place is so busy. So many people come from outside.'

While Shanghai has 14 million residents with a local *hukou*, at least another 10 million migrants reside in the city. According to Wenli, 'People don't know each other, so they don't take any risks.'

I asked him how he had gone from not wanting to be a teacher in Shaoyang to being a teacher in Shanghai.

'First I went to Kunming, because our college has many links to that place. I thought I could get a job in a company. But it was very hard; for three months I tried, but the competition was too strong.'

Increasing competition among graduates has meant that even the best students are often forced to look for work outside their own province. Between 1998 and 2008 the number of undergraduates increased fivefold, which has led to a corresponding increase in graduate unemployment. A recent study found that only 68 per cent in 2009 found work, compared to 94 per cent in 1996.[5] The poor living conditions that many have to endure – often in small rooms at the edge of the urban area – have led to them being referred to as an 'ant tribe'.

Finding a job in China often depends on one's contacts, which in some cases can be as simple as having a friend already working in a factory or company. But although Wenli's participation in the gala performances meant he was held in high esteem by the college leaders, they hadn't been much help to him after he left.

'Maybe if I had stayed in Shaoyang, the leaders would know some people. But Kunming is too far. They do not have *guanxi* there.'

Guanxi can simply refer to a person's contacts, but can also indicate the way they were obtained. When used in this second sense, *guanxi* often connotes corruption. In 2010, China was 78th out of 178 countries on Transparency International's Corruption Perceptions Index, which focuses on public-sector corruption. The Chinese government does not deny the existence of the problem, and regularly announces anti-corruption initiatives, which usually involve the indictment of high-profile figures. One of the most notable contemporary examples of these was the dismissal of Bo

Xilai in 2012. The charismatic former Party secretary of Chongqing city was once thought a candidate for a top government position, but was sentenced to life imprisonment for corruption and abuse of power. Though few doubted the corruption charges, there was also public sympathy for the mayor, mainly due to the fact that he'd made some efforts to reduce the gap between rich and poor in the city (including making it easier for migrants to gain an urban *hukou*). Since then Xi Jinping has launched an aggressive campaign against corruption as part of the Chinese Dream. Though undoubtedly real – many senior officials have been jailed – some saw it as a way for Xi to consolidate his authority.

One problem with trying to assess the scale of corruption in China, at least at a low level, is that there's often a grey area about what someone expects when they ask for a favour. Even if the request seems legitimate, it can open the door to more problematic demands. In Shaoyang, many of my colleagues asked me to do favours for their friends, most typically visiting a local school. Though I was usually glad to do so, after the visit my colleague's friend (often a local businessman) would take me for a meal, get me drunk, then ask me for a much bigger favour. Most wanted me to become a private tutor for their children, but I was also asked to help promote their school by appearing on local TV or posing for photos for its prospectus. In most cases, my refusal was taken gracefully, but there were instances when it was mistaken for a negotiating strategy, prompting a flurry of gifts, and once with a red envelope full of money being thrust at me. When I refused, the man stuffed it into my pocket. I tried giving it back, but the man refused to take it, so I put the envelope on the ground, which made him actually roar with anger. I was later told by a friend that this was such an insult that the man would have beaten me if I had been Chinese.

The complexities of *guanxi* were not the only reason Wenli didn't want the college's help. He asked if I remembered a teacher called Mr Liu.

'Vaguely,' I said, and conjured up a man with a mischievous face who ignored me unless he needed help with phrasal verbs.

'Mr Liu organised many of the performances. We went to his house often, sometimes in the evening, so he could teach us the dances. But he also put his arms round us. Some classmates said he tried to kiss them.'

'Was that true?'

Wenli hesitated. 'Mr Liu was my friend. But I think it was true. He did not do this with me, but I believe my classmates.'

Wenli eventually found a job in Kunming after a friend from his home town told him there was a job in the company where he worked.

'I went to see the boss of the company and he agreed. The salary was low, but I didn't care. I worked very hard, and it was boring, I had to check a lot of forms, some in English, some in Chinese. But I was glad to have a job.'

After three years Wenli left Kunming and went to Guilin (capital of Guangxi province, and a nine-hour bus ride from Shaoyang). He went into business with one of his childhood friends – doing what he wouldn't say, only that there was a lot of money involved – but soon realised that their business was illegal. When Wenli told his partner he wanted to stop, he was locked in a room. His mobile phone and wallet were taken, and two guards were posted outside the door. When, on the third day, he escaped through a toilet window, he was pursued by the angry guards.

'I had no money, no phone. I was just running, but then I remembered a coin my friend gave me when I left college. It was in a small pocket of my trousers for years; I never took it out, not even when I washed them. It was only one yuan, but it was enough to make a call. I phoned my friend who works in the Kunming police department, and he said he would call his uncle, who is the police chief in Guilin.'

'But the men were still chasing you?'

'Yes, but when they caught me I told them about the police. Then they went away.'

He smiled, then said, 'After I left Guilin I heard about this job and I came here. Now I am a… a *niu bi*.'

'A what?'

'A cow's vagina. It means that I am someone who is up-and-coming. If I stay here four more years I will get a *hukou* for Shanghai, which means my kids can go to school here. Or maybe I will sell it. On the black market it is worth 200,000 yuan.'

Apart from its more dramatic details, Wenli's story echoed that of many other migrant workers in China, who often jump from one job to another in an attempt to improve their salary and conditions. A recent survey of young graduates in six major Chinese cities found that 30 per cent changed their jobs at least once a year, and 70 per cent changed their jobs every three years.[6] While the same is true of young graduates in the US, the tendency in China represents a more drastic shift, given that until the late 1990s most people tended to stay in the same public-sector job.

After lunch we took a stroll round his neighbourhood. A group of old women were walking a posse of small white dogs that had pink, protruding tongues and looked incredibly pleased. When we got to the end of the block, Wenli realised he had forgotten his bag of medicine. He sprinted back to the restaurant, and when he returned, held up the bag like a trophy.

'What's in there?'

'Medicine. It was made by an old man from Sichuan who is very wise.'

When I asked Wenli how his former classmates were doing, he said he knew of three girls now working in Changsha, two boys in Nanjing and another in Guangzhou. I knew most of the students by the English names they used in class, whereas Wenli only knew them by their actual Chinese names. Most of our conversations about them went like this:

'What about Tommy? Do you know where he is?'

'Who is Tommy?'

'He was in your class. He was from Xiangtan and was good at basketball.'

'Was he tall?'

'I think so.'

'Oh, I know him. A very fast runner. I don't know where he is.'

We walked till the end of the block, and then there were no more shops and houses, just an expanse of rubble. It was as if there had been a localised earthquake. The one surviving wall was marked with a large, spray-painted Chinese character which I had seen on the walls of many houses, shops and restaurants over the years. It was *chai*, which means 'tear down' or 'raze'. The building was condemned.

Waves of demolitions have swept through China's major cities since the 1990s, resulting in an almost total reconfiguration of urban space. Old neighbourhoods with narrow streets and court-yard houses have been replaced by shopping malls, skyscrapers, apartment blocks and six-lane roads. In Shanghai over 18,000 households were destroyed to make room for the 2010 Expo, for which six new underground lines were dug and a new airport terminal constructed.[7] Some critics suggested it was just a way for the Shanghai municipal government to reclaim the land so that it could be redeveloped at great profit.

Land is one of the most valuable commodities in China. While there's no private land *ownership* in China, the question of who has the right to *use* a plot of land is more complicated. One can own a house but not control the use of the land it is built on. There are different rules for how land can be used according to whether it's classified as 'rural' or 'urban' (a classification that can reflect which authority controls it, rather than whether it's in a city or the countryside). The right to use 'rural' land is controlled by village collectives, whereas 'urban' land is controlled by municipal authorities. Since 1988 there's been a market for land designated as 'urban', which allows 70-year leases for residential properties, and 50-year leases for commercial ones. Urban authorities can decide to transfer the usage rights for a piece of land to a private property-development company – who will generally build either offices or apartment blocks – and there's usually little residents can do about it, though by law all are supposed to receive compensation and/or replacement housing.

The main reason municipal authorities authorise these land transfers (and the consequent evictions of their citizens) is that they make a lot of money for the city. Since 1994, when the government stopped most direct funding to cities and towns, officials have had to find other ways to pay for the wide range of services they provide residents (offering a further incentive for them to deny people without a local *hukou* access to education and healthcare). In addition to the money earned from land deals, many apparently 'private' land-development companies are actually owned by municipalities (and in some cases by the officials themselves). While the city authorities do have some responsibilities, such as paying compensation, relocation costs, clearing the site and ensuring infrastructure is in place for new construction, even after this the profits are substantial. A joint study by Michigan State University and Beijing's Renmin University found that cities make on average 40 times what they pay in compensation;[8] for some municipalities, such as Changsha (the provincial capital of Hunan), almost 100 per cent of their finances come from land deals. This is apparently enough to allow most urban authorities to meet their budgetary shortfall, though the actual level of debt of China's cities is unknown – a study by Tsinghua University in 2015 found that only 1 per cent of local governments make their finances public.[9]

Given the opacity of their finances, it's hard to answer the vital question of whether China's cities can afford to pay for healthcare, education and other social services for 250 million new residents, let alone make these cities more environmentally friendly. A World Bank report from 2013 estimated it would cost around $16,000 for each new urban *hukou* holder.[10] Even if only 20 million new urban residents were created every year (as is planned), this would still require an estimated additional $8.2 billion to be spent every year.

Unsurprisingly, many people have been unhappy about being evicted from their homes. While most protests in the 1990s in China were in response to heavy rural taxes, since the 2000s 'land grabs', by both rural and urban authorities, have been the main cause of dissent. The most notable recent example was the protests that erupted at Wukan village in Guangdong province in September 2011, caused by local land being sold to property developers.[11] These led to attacks on government buildings, officials being expelled from the village, and Wukan then being besieged by the police, who blocked food from entering the village. Though the dispute was eventually settled, it clearly frightened the authorities, who imposed a media blackout on the area, no doubt fearing it might serve as an example to other communities with similar grievances.

Faced with official indifference and lack of legal recourse, some residents have been driven to despair. In September 2013 He Mingqing, a 42-year-old rice farmer from Chenzhou, in southeast Hunan, locked himself in his home when the demolition team arrived. The local government wanted to level his house, and the rest of the village, to build a park. While the farmer had been offered compensation, he had no other means of earning a living once his land was gone. When officials forced his door open with a crowbar, he poured petrol over his head then set himself on fire. Though badly burned, he survived. Local officials denied responsibility, claiming the house had been illegally built and that his self-immolation had been an attempt to get more money. He may have been inspired by the death of Zhou Lijun, a 47-year-old woman, also from Hunan, who had burned herself to death several months before in protest at her eviction, and whose family received more than $570,000 in compensation.[12] Whether or not He's protest was an attempt to imitate her actions, it certainly spoke volumes about his desperation. The same could be said of the more than 50 people who have set themselves on fire in other parts of China since 2009, or the 13 people who drank pesticide in Tiananmen Square in December 2013 for the same reason.[13]

According to Wenli, the Expo demolitions in Shanghai had also been very unpopular. 'Some people were angry. They said they have lived here all their life and do not want to go because of an exhibition that is for rich people. They said they cannot afford to live in the city and must go outside.'

We walked for another block, then the buildings resumed. I stopped to buy miniature mangos. As I smelt their almost-poisonous sweetness, Wenli said, 'I had three girlfriends this year, and they were all bad. Mean and very crazy. They were all rat girls.'

'Why do you call them that?'

'Because they were born in the year of the rat.' He sighed. 'My relatives say I must get married soon, but I tell them it's better to wait. But things have changed a lot. Now a girl will have sex before she gets married, but if she has sex, she often wants to get married. But if you do not, it is OK.'

We turned off the street into a residential compound where the air smelt of honeysuckle. The apartments were five storeys of white-tiled concrete with red numbers painted on their sides. We went inside one and climbed two flights of stairs, then Wenli opened a door. We stepped into a small hallway, took our shoes off and pushed our feet into fluffy slippers. The flat had a lounge, two bedrooms, a kitchen and bathroom. Wenli was certainly not one of the 'ant tribe'. I knew teachers who had worked for 20 years in Shaoyang Teachers' College and lived in worse conditions.

Wenli went into the kitchen and filled a large saucepan with water. He put it on the stove, then said, 'I must cook the medicine.'

He opened the red bag and took out a second made of thick paper. It contained various brown items with a dry, pungent smell. I couldn't tell if they were rocks, plants or the innards of some creature.

'What's that?' I said and poked what looked to be an ear.

'I do not know,' he said, then smelt it. He touched it with his tongue.

'Fungus. And that' – he pointed – 'is bark.'

I picked up what looked to be a fossilised pomegranate. 'And this?'

'That is the house of wasps.'

'Really? Are you going to eat that?'

'Of course not. I will put it on my skin. But when I was a boy I knocked down bees' nests. We ate the honey, and sometimes we ate the larvae too. I think I was very wild then.'

He emptied the bag into the pan, then brought the water to the boil. I asked how much longer he planned to stay in Shanghai.

'Till I get the household registration. And I want to get a lot of money.'

'What will you do with it?'

'When I was younger, I wanted to travel the world on my own. Now I only want a home, a wife, some children and a dog. But I don't want to work all my life. I want to stop when I am 45 or 50. I would like to live on a mountain, maybe learn about medicine so I can treat people for free.'

He stirred the mixture, then turned the heat down. At the time, I thought his dream was romantic, but totally genuine. This is a powerful story in China: the country boy who comes to the city and finds success, but whose heart remains in his home town.

But next day, as I sat on the train to Hunan, I remembered Wenli rubbing the medicine onto his shoulders and back. He had to leave it on for two hours, which meant us staying at home. We sat and drank beer. After three bottles Wenli said, 'Do you like Nintendo?'

'Yes,' I said, and so we played Super Mario Brothers together. At first it was like we were playing separately; but slowly, with the loss of much life, we learnt to cooperate.

We had just beaten the boss monster at the end of the third level when his mobile rang.

'Excuse me, it's my uncle,' he said and started speaking, first in standard Chinese, then mixing it with Shaoyang dialect. The latter sounded jagged, almost crude, whereas the standard parts were smooth. It was like when I used to hear my students speaking Chinese among themselves. Students who were sweet and demure in English could also be foul-mouthed bullies who drove their meeker classmates to tears. In the different languages they had two completely different personas, but there was no contradiction. Like Wenli, they chose to be both.

*

Wenli hadn't made it to the top of the waterfall, but he was definitely rising up. Though this was impressive, I didn't find it surprising, given his confidence and ability. What I couldn't understand was how Xiao Long, a student who seemed to have at least as promising a future, had ended up in a small rural school. I wanted to know what he'd done differently to Wenli, whether he'd faced particular obstacles.

Xiao Long's excellent English was in no small part due to the fact that he had been good friends with the foreign teachers who had taught in Shaoyang before me. He had incredible self-belief: there were many students who worked harder and were more knowledge-able about the language, but they lacked the necessary confidence to approach a native speaker (even when he or she was their teacher). Soon after graduation he started work in a junior high school on top of a mountain, but he was adamant that this was temporary. He had bigger plans.

After Xiao Long had been working for a few months, he bought a shiny maroon motorbike. He used to turn up at my flat without warning on Friday evenings, usually with the intention of spending the weekend with me. Often I was glad to see him, because unlike most of my students he wasn't intimidated or shy around me. He didn't bombard me with questions like, 'Can you use chopsticks?' or 'Why is London so foggy?' He preferred to talk about a British girl called Zara who had taught in the college before me, for whom he still nursed an infatuation. His dream was not just of having a good job with a high salary and the chance of going abroad, but also having a foreign wife. Though he often speculated about the qualities of women from other countries, all these musings led back to Zara.

When I left Shaoyang in 2001 Xiao Long was about to go to Guangdong province to look for work. Given his confidence, and fluency in English, I expected he'd have little trouble. The following year I got an email saying he had found an excellent job, and after that heard nothing from him other than an email three years later wishing me a Happy Christmas. I had planned to visit him in Guangzhou, and was surprised when he emailed back to say he was in Shaoyang. We arranged to meet at the train station, and he seemed to be looking forward to it. 'BIG REUNION!' he texted, followed by 'IT WILL BE XMAS!'

Unfortunately, I was a little rusty at reading a Chinese railway timetable. I thought I could change trains in Hengyang, the second largest city in Hunan, but when I arrived it was 10 p.m. and the next train to Shaoyang wasn't until 5 a.m. The station was on the edge of town, and there were no hotels nearby. I was contemplating putting all my clothes on and trying to sleep in a corner, when a man and woman in their early thirties asked where I was going. When I told them, she said, 'So are we.' I asked her how much she wanted. She looked at my clothes, then suggested a price. I suggested a sum that was smaller, but still too much, and this satisfied us both.

Soon we were speeding along an unlit, poorly surfaced road whose main traffic was juggernauts with lights that blinded me as they hurtled towards us. I wanted to close my eyes, but didn't; I thought if I saw the crash coming I might be able to do something in those final seconds – such as throwing myself to the floor – that would mean the difference between severe injury and death. My only distraction was a succession of text messages from Xiao Long. He was trying to guess the identity of the gift I had brought him. 'MUSIC PLAYER?', 'DVD?', and, finally, 'SOMETHING SPECIAL?'

It was in keeping with our last meeting ten years ago. Then I was supposed to be leaving Shaoyang in 20 minutes, and still hadn't worked out what to do with the many kind but cumbersome leaving presents I had been given. I was considering splitting up a tea set when Xiao Long said, 'Maybe I can help you?'

'Do you want them?'

'Of course not. But I think I can get money for them.' He picked up the needlework sampler featuring two grey kittens. 'Not a lot,' he said, then looked at me reprovingly, as if I had thought this kitsch item priceless. 'But a little is still good!'

'What if you can't sell them?'

'I will give them to a woman. You know, women really like gifts.'

Xiao Long's final barrage of texts came after I had been en route for two hours. 'WHERE R U?' was quickly followed by 'HURRY UP', then 'I CANNOT WAIT'. The last was worrying, as he had arranged my hotel. I texted that I would arrive in under half an hour. 'HAD TO GO SEE YOU TOMORROW!' was his reply. My emotional return to Shaoyang after almost a decade began with me being dropped off outside a building I didn't recognise, on a street I didn't know, at one o'clock in the morning.

I stood for a moment, then began to walk. When a taxi appeared, I stopped it and asked the driver to take me to the best hotel in Shaoyang. She nodded and asked no further questions. As we drove,

I recognised nothing, but couldn't tell if this was because things had changed or because I had forgotten. Then we were crossing the Shao River, passing four giant statues of rhinos. For centuries their task has been to keep a green dragon trapped in the river.

We turned off the road and went through a grand red gate I'd never noticed before. We drove between dark apartment blocks, then stopped in front of a hotel with a lighted fountain outside. Inside, the lobby was vast, its walls covered with velvet and mirrors. The floor was marble and almost all the guests were middle-aged or elderly men wearing well-cut suits. I had not known that such an opulent hotel existed in Shaoyang; it made me wonder if the rest of the city had been similarly transformed.

But next morning I walked through streets I recognised. The roads were better and many shops now had doors, but most of the buildings were still only two or three storeys high and in a worn condition. On the pavements people sold tights and socks or peeled pineapples. Wild dogs ran in and out of traffic. There were no shopping centres or multinational chains; the nearest thing was a faux McDonald's called Peter Burger.

Things hadn't changed much in the college, either. There were new dormitories and teaching buildings, but the classrooms were the same. The long rows of desks and benches were still bolted to the floor, the teacher's desk still raised up on a concrete platform. As for the blackboards, I wondered if they were the same ones I had written on. They were topped with slogans in coloured plastic like 'Better Every Day!' and 'We can have the Moon!'

The English department had moved to another building. When I walked into its office I saw a woman in her early sixties wearing black slacks and a maroon tunic buttoned all the way up. This was Dean Chen, my old boss, who I had liked because although she was never particularly helpful, she wasn't obstructive either. As I watched her mouth open and eyes widen, I felt like one of those long-dead characters in a soap opera who return in order to boost ratings. Only then did I consider that it might have been courteous to inform them I was thinking of popping in after a ten-year absence.

After an exchange of pleasantries, Dean Chen asked why I had come back. I paused. 'Curiosity', though close to the truth, didn't seem an adequate reason. 'I'm doing some research about English-language teaching in China,' I said, and when this lie was accepted, added, 'Would it be possible to speak to some of the teachers?'

'Of course,' said Dean Chen, then left the room. I checked my phone and saw I had seven messages from Xiao Long.

Dean Chen never returned, but after a while a young teacher came and introduced herself as 'Sunny'. Her English had a mild American lilt, the result of her spending the previous summer in California. We talked about problems in the classroom, the main one being that the exams were still designed to test the students' written English but that their ability to speak wasn't assessed. As a result, students tended to direct their efforts more towards the former.

We were interrupted by a knock on the door. As we turned Xiao Long said, 'There you are!' He was wearing a black-and-white-striped sweater under a bright orange jacket. His hair had receded so much he looked like a middle-aged Mao Zedong.

Sunny had to go and teach. As soon as she left the room, Xiao Long leaned close and whispered, 'Now I know why you don't answer your phone. You have been making a *good* friend.'

When I protested that I had only just met her, he said, 'This is a good chance for you. Why not have a try?'

'She's married.'

'That is no problem. In fact, you have a better chance. It means she will know more about the pleasure of sex.'

He nodded, looking very pleased, as if this were something he had arranged. Then he grew serious.

'But I must tell you that you look much older. Really. You should take more care of yourself.'

I laughed, but must have looked wounded, because he added, 'You know, we are friends, so it is OK if I say this to you.'

'Shall we go into town?' I said.

We spent the rest of the morning looking for people and places that no longer existed. A long street of old houses by the river had been replaced by a stretch of karaoke bars that doubled as brothels. My favourite restaurant – a two-storey wooden house where it was best to keep one's feet off the floor because of the rats – was now a rubbish-compacting plant. When I knocked on the door of the man who used to develop my films in his kitchen (and only bothered with negatives he thought were interesting) we were told he had died. Such changes were in no way profound, and only to be expected; what surprised me was how reluctant my memories were to be updated. I had been honing my image of the town for a decade. Although I had come to find out what had changed, what I looked for, and longed for, were the things that had not. Of these, there were few: the Ming-dynasty tower with grass growing from its walls; the old red teahouse overlooking the river; the temple on a hill whose lights I used to see at night. And of course, the Shao River, its waters still the colour of a jade milkshake.

'There are many changes here,' said Xiao Long. 'Conditions are much better. Ten years ago, I could not stand it.'

'That was when you went to Guangzhou?'

'Yes, and I got a very good job. I worked in a factory that made circuit boards. I had to check the specifications on each order. I worked hard, but the pay was very good.'

'So what happened? Why did you leave?'

He sighed. 'For a year, it was wonderful. But then I made a mistake. I got a number wrong on an order, and they made many boards that were useless.'

'Did they fire you?

31

'No, but I was so embarrassed that I left the job. I came back here, and I didn't tell anyone what happened. I told people I preferred to be a teacher.'

He paused as a lorry clattered by, packed with pigs whose snouts poked between the bars. It wasn't social or institutional boundaries that had defeated him, just his sense of shame.

We walked on. Xiao Long asked if I ever played the stock market. When I shook my head, he said, 'That is good. I used to play but I lost half my fortune because I didn't know about it. With the rest, I bought my car. It is very important for me, because my school is outside the city, about 30 kilometres from here. If you have some free time, I will take you.'

His car was blue and tiny. As we left the city it started to rain, initially a light drizzle, then hard enough to bring the blossom off the trees. On the outskirts of Shaoyang the houses were two-storey, flat-roofed buildings covered in white tiles. But as the city segued into country, their ancestors appeared. Most were built of faded red brick and topped with sloping grey roofs. There were also older houses made from blocks of yellow mud. Slogans were painted on some of their walls, most of which were adverts for mobile phone companies, though there were also political messages. One of them read, 'Not sending your kids to school is illegal!' Another reminded us that 'Stability is the number one responsibility.'

Xiao Long said he loved driving his car, but had been unable to for a while because his doctor had advised against it.

'How come?'

'I had an operation on my haemorrhoids because they were very bad. But now it is wonderful to go fast again,' he said, then sounded the car horn. Ahead of us a group of dogs leaped from the road. They streamed down the side of the hill, then separated in the fields. Against the deep red soil their coats were a pale blur.

The road rose and fell. We passed two women clutching limp chickens. Ducks swam on a pond.

I asked Xiao Long how he felt about ending up as a teacher. I knew it wasn't a sensitive question.

'It is not what I wanted,' he said. 'I want a more comfortable life. A teacher must work very hard. When I first came back, I taught in the junior school on the mountain. The children were very wild, like animals. They were hard to control. One day I lost my temper with a boy and kicked him. He fell over and his classmates laughed and for weeks he was upset. I felt very bad. I have not done that again.'

Xiao Long taught in a senior middle school, which covers ages 16–18. We arrived at break time, when the students were outside, kicking balls, chatting, listening to music, reading out loud from their textbooks. As we approached, a boy on the top floor shouted, 'America, America!' After that we stumbled through an auditory crossfire – 'Hello,' but also 'Cool, man!', 'Hurry up!' and 'Look at the tomato!'

'You are their first foreigner,' said Xiao Long. 'They are very excited.'

As we climbed the concrete steps, the voices fell away. Heads bobbed in and out of doorways. All I heard were whispers, plosive sounds of excitement. When Xiao Long opened a metal door, it was clear where the voices had gone. They had gathered in the classroom, massing, acquiring more decibels than 50 small throats could otherwise muster. The students sat at small wooden desks, wearing coats and jackets because the classroom was unheated. A foot-high tower of books rose from each desk, the textbooks the students had to learn for the *gaokao*, also known as the National Higher Education Entrance Examination. In 2010, around ten million students were competing for approximately 6.6 million places in colleges and universities. The exams take place over three intensive days in June, and though there are regional variations, Chinese, mathematics and a foreign language (usually English) are compulsory. Students are also required to write 800-character essays on such abstruse topics as 'Why chase mice when there are fish to eat?' and 'What is light reading?' There are also province-specific questions. In 2009, Hunan's question was the single word 'Morning'.

Rural schools generally have poorer facilities and lower teaching standards, placing their students at an obvious disadvantage in the competition for higher education places. This is further compounded by the fact that rural middle-school headmasters can't recommend students to the top universities. As a result, rural students are seven times less likely to attend college than those from urban areas, and eleven times less likely to attend one of the elite schools. These inequalities won't encourage a greater flow of educated young people from the countryside to the cities.

Once the students settled down, they began asking questions, most of which were better versions of the ones my students used to ask. They still wanted to know about London, but instead of asking whether it was foggy, and home to ladies and gentlemen, they said things like, 'Tell me about the River Thames' or 'What buildings do you like?' Instead of asking if I liked China, they asked *what* I liked about it. This was probably attributable to Xiao Long, who despite his reservations was obviously a good teacher. When he spoke the students were attentive; they seemed used to hearing him speak English.

I answered the students' questions until the lesson bell rang. The students waved and yelled a polyphonic goodbye. Xiao Long led me through a door at the back of the classroom into a small room with a concrete floor and bars on its windows whose furniture consisted of a single bed, two tables piled with books and papers, a small sink, a two-ring cooker and a desk. On this there was a computer whose desktop photo was of a very different room, a spacious, well-furnished lounge with ornaments on its coffee table and flowers in vases. I realised his screen saver was a picture of how he wished his room looked.

We sat and talked and drank green tea from plastic cups. He asked if I believed in zombies, and when I said no, he nodded, and apropos of nothing, said he was married and had a child. When I acted surprised, he looked slightly ashamed, perhaps thinking of the many times he had spoken of Zara.

'You know, this is our custom in China. A man is supposed to get married when he is in his twenties. If he does not, people will say there is something wrong with him.'

I asked him how he'd met his wife.

'Someone introduced us,' he said, by which I guessed he meant a matchmaker.

Xiao Long refilled our cups with hot water from a red thermos flask. Behind him, at the window, two boys waved at me. He blew on his tea, then said, 'If you know about me, you can know everything about China.'

At the time, this made me laugh: it seemed conceited of him to portray himself as an Everyman. But later, as we drove back to Shaoyang, I realised he was more typical than Wenli. The carp that becomes a dragon must be the exception. Just because my students had had new opportunities, that hadn't made it easier to be from rural families. It was only due to a happy combination of good fortune, personal ambition and perhaps *guanxi* that Wenli was not teaching in a school near where he'd been born. As for Xiao Long, though he had probably had the best chance he was going to get, he refused to give up.

'Next year I will get a new car. I have a good chance to make some money on a copper business. If I get enough, I will visit you in London,' he said, and pressed the accelerator.

2

BUTTERING THE TIGER

My students in Shaoyang knew how to achieve their dreams. 'I will go to Guangzhou,' they said, often in a slightly arch manner, as if they had been the first to think of this idea. In theory, there was nothing wrong with this plan – there were lots of jobs in that region. The problem was that most of the students weren't qualified to be anything except teachers, and had no experience of working in a factory or company. They weren't alone in having this problem – the same tends to be true of most young rural migrants. Finding a job often depends on having a friend or relative already working in a company who can recommend them (and sometimes by pretending to have relevant work experience). Both Xiao Long and Wenli had found jobs because they'd known someone who could vouch for them.

From Shaoyang I took an overnight train to visit another former student. The following afternoon I stood outside Guangzhou South station, watching people stream in and out of the station. It was hot and the air smelt of petrol; the haze and bustle made everything seem liminal. I was waiting for Da Ming, one of Wenli's classmates, who I remembered as being bookish and diligent. We had often eaten lunch together, and I had visited his family home in the countryside several times. We had also worked closely together on an English-language newspaper for the college that featured articles such as 'Why men are pigs', 'Our Mother, the Sun' and 'How to improve your mouth'. I remembered him having a strong sense of right and wrong, and being critical of many things in China, especially corruption. In the final exam I asked his class to give an example of an extended metaphor. He wrote:

> The English Department is the second largest department in our school. But I dislike it. Always, I think it is a world of animals. The leaders, the cruel tigers, always roar at the students to follow their orders. The members of the students union are foxes, always buttering the tiger. The leaders must be sucked and their hides brushed by those tick-eating birds. Some students, who got a scholarship, are just like the hen, cackling now and then. Those who want to study their speciality are like bees, never doing anything to set the world on fire.

As I waited outside the station I scanned the crowd for a tall, unassuming boy with acne scars and thick glasses. When a round-headed man with bristly hair said my name in a nasal voice, my disbelief must have been apparent.

'It's Da Ming,' he said, and I said, 'I know,' but wasn't entirely convinced.

'You look the same,' he said. 'But I have got very fat. Now I look older than you!'

This was, unfortunately, not true.

We walked past a rank of red taxis whose drivers beckoned to us. When I asked Da Ming if we were taking the underground, he said, 'No need. I have a car.'

'Really?'

'Yes. I must have, I need it for my business.'

Though I had known doctors, teachers and heads of academic departments when I lived in Shaoyang ten years before, none of them had owned a car. Even the president of the teachers' college had to share one with the Party secretary. While I knew that car ownership had greatly increased over the last decade, it was still surprising to me that Da Ming was successful enough to be able to own one. He'd been a modest, reflective young man who didn't seem to have the calculating streak necessary for commerce. It wasn't until I saw his black Toyota SUV that I realised he was doing very well. I asked Da Ming what kind of business he was involved in.

'I have a factory that makes mobile phone accessories. Some things for BlackBerry too.'

'Are you the manager?'

'No, it is all mine. I have about 60 workers. Business was bad for the first few years. I lost 1.7 million yuan, about $250,000. But now things are very good, because relations with America are better. We are selling in Target stores. And we have orders from many places. The biggest was $200,000 from South America.'

We crawled through traffic, then drove up an expressway ramp. Soon we were driving through fields where the new rice was a shade of green brighter than lime – it was like the colour of plant blood.

I was glad Da Ming was doing well, but I had read about appalling working conditions in factories in Guangzhou involving long hours and poor safety training. One study published by the Shanghai Academy of Social Sciences found that factory workers in the region lost or broke about 40,000 fingers on the job every year.[1] It was hard not to imagine Da Ming's factory as some Stygian basement full of machines with a high maiming potential.

Da Ming said, 'Do you like fish? Because there is a lot of good fish in Guangzhou.'

I said that I liked fish.

'You know, Nick, the food here is different to Shaoyang. They do not use the chilli pepper so much. And I have got used to this, I have lived here five years now. When I go back to visit my relatives in Shaoyang the food is too spicy for me. Maybe I am not a Shaoyang person any more.'

'Does that bother you?'

'Now I have my family here, I think this is my home.'

'Your parents are here?'

'I bought them a flat. They say it is too hot here, especially in summer, but they do not have a choice.'

Though there is a long tradition of obedience to parents in China, the wealth that some rural migrants have found in the cities has disrupted the familial balance of power.

His parents' flat overlooked a vegetable market that was closing when we arrived. Da Ming unlocked a gate and we climbed three flights of stairs. When he unlocked a second gate, a little boy in an orange T-shirt ran down to him. Da Ming picked him up.

'This is my son; he is a naughty boy. But he is very clever. He understands a lot of things. He can already use the DVD player, which my mother cannot.'

We went inside and Da Ming introduced me to his wife. She was a short, pretty woman wearing a yellow sweatshirt and black slacks, an outfit that would not have been out of place in Shaoyang ten years ago. I asked Da Ming how they had met.

'She was working in the same company as me. Now she runs 70 per cent of the business. She is also my accountant. She is much cleverer than me!'

He smiled at her, and she smiled back. It was obvious, from this long look, how much they loved each other.

'My father does the cooking,' he said, and as if on cue his father came out of the kitchen with a bowl of shrimp. We sat down around a small table with five dishes of food on it – shrimp, eggs, a whole fish, some kind of spinach, hunks of beef on the bone. And though they were now living in a new place, with more money at their disposal, it struck me that we were eating a similar meal to the ones we'd had when they were still living in Shaoyang.

After dinner, Da Ming played with his son while his mother peeled me an apple whose peel came off in a single spiral. There were a few attempts to get the boy to speak English to me ('Say "uncle"!

"Uncle"!'), but the child preferred to communicate by hitting me with a toy helicopter.

Da Ming's mobile rang, and after a short exchange – during which he made sounds of disapproval – he turned to me and said, 'I am sorry, I must go to the factory, there is a problem. If you are tired I can take you to your hotel.'

I told him I was fine, and was very much looking forward to seeing the factory.

It was only nine o'clock, but the streets through which we drove were deserted. Da Ming asked if I had ever been to France. When I told him I had, he asked if I liked it. Before I could answer he said, 'I went there and did not like it. People were very rude and I felt uncomfortable. It was the same in Germany. I think people were against me because I am Chinese.'

In Shaoyang we had often spoken about foreign countries, how many I had been to, what they were like. There had been an air of unreality to these conversations, because he had never been outside of Hunan, and if he ended up as a high-school teacher that wasn't likely to change.

'Before I left China, I didn't like it and hated the government. Now I like the government because they help farmers a lot. They got rid of many taxes, and it only costs a little for medical insurance.'

We stopped outside a large grey building with no windows at ground level. We got out, then Da Ming unlocked a metal door. Inside was a narrow hallway with a concrete floor on which sat a black dog with short fur and very black eyes. The dog began to growl. Then it opened its mouth, made a muffled bark, and trotted over to Da Ming. He picked it up and said, 'This is the factory dog. He came here a year ago, and now he lives here.' The dog flexed a paw then yawned.

Da Ming pointed to a door on the right. 'This is the dormitory where some workers sleep.' He pushed the door open a few inches and I saw two rows of bunk beds, on which three men were sleeping. I noticed a sink in the corner, and a door that led to a toilet.

'Let's go to my office,' said Da Ming, and we went upstairs. I asked him where the rest of the workers were.

'Most like to stay outside. If they stay in the dormitory it is free, but if they stay outside, I give them an extra 300 yuan.'

'What about if they have family here? Do you still give them money?'

'No,' he said, and switched on a light. I saw rows of sewing machines, bolts of cloth, piles of vinyl and leather. 'But most are from far away, mainly Guangxi or Sichuan province.'

'How much do you pay them?'

'It depends. Between 1,000 and 1,300 yuan a month.'

'Is that low?'

'It is average. But I try to make the conditions good. In the past, maybe some employers didn't treat their workers well. But now, if we want to keep our workers, we must.'

Before the global financial crash of 2008, China's manufacturing sector had seemed to have a boundless demand for labour. Raw materials came into its ports, destined to be turned into consumer items for export by the hundreds of millions working in factories. But the fragility of this arrangement became apparent after the crash. Global recession led to a drop in demand for Chinese goods, causing many factories to close. There's no consensus about how many lost their jobs, with estimates varying between 20 and 50 million people. In many places this led to riots and protests over unpaid wages. The most dramatic incident took place at a steel plant in Tonghua, in Jilin province, where 30,000 workers rioted at the lay-offs.[2] Protestors blocked roads and smashed police vehicles, then broke into the office of the chief executive of the steel plant, who they then beat to death.

In Guangdong, most laid-off workers had no choice but to go back to their home towns. Faced with the new uncertainty about whether there would be work available, many opted not to return. In 2009, for the first time in many years, there was a drop in the number of people travelling after Chinese New Year. The *People's Daily* newspaper announced that 20 million had chosen not to go back to the coastal cities – many went to look for work in cities in the interior.[3]

According to Da Ming, this relative labour shortage meant that workers had more bargaining power.

'You can cheat someone once, but then everyone will know and they will not work for you.'

I was almost persuaded that he wasn't running a sweatshop, but then he added, 'If companies are treating workers badly, they must be foreign ones.'

Da Ming was referring to the spate of suicides at the Foxconn factories in nearby Shenzhen.[4] Foxconn, a Taiwanese electronics manufacturer that makes the iPad, iPhone, Kindle, PlayStation and Xbox, is the largest private company in China, employing around a million workers. The suicides were blamed on long working hours, insufficient overtime pay and frequent workplace accidents. Subsequent investigations found some evidence for these claims, though Foxconn had its defenders. After inspecting a number of factories, the president of the Fair Labour Association, an organisation that promotes adherence to international and national labour laws, noted that conditions were 'way, way above average of the norm [in China]'.[5]

I didn't want to think the worst of Da Ming, but the brief glimpse I'd had of the shabby-looking dormitories in the factory didn't inspire confidence. I also wondered where his start-up money had come from. His parents were teachers, and to my knowledge he had no rich relatives. I couldn't imagine a bank giving a big loan to a graduate of Shaoyang Teachers' College.

As Da Ming unlocked his office, I said, 'So how did you get the money for this place?'

He turned on the lights and I saw a long room whose centre had been partitioned into four cubes, each with a desk and computer.

Da Ming asked me to sit, then said, 'I got it from a customer in the company where I worked before.'

'Was that your first job?'

'No, after I left Shaoyang I taught for one year. Then I came here and got a job in that company as a translator. They do a lot of foreign trade. Then I began to know about business, and so I changed my job in that company to sales.'

'How did you manage to do that? Did you have *guanxi* with someone?'

'No, I am just a good worker, I work very, very hard. You know, in Guangzhou it is not important if you have *guanxi*. The first thing is your ability. I spoke to this customer in Egypt about many things, he was like a teacher. He got me my first order.'

Da Ming said he had to make a phone call, and went out of the room. As I waited for him to return I wondered how he could have lost so much money in his first year and survived. It wasn't entirely suspicious, but it seemed in need of explanation.

When Da Ming came back he looked tired. We went downstairs, said goodnight to the dog, then got in the car. As we drove off I saw a man squatting next to a small fire on the pavement, feeding its flames with pieces of paper. Da Ming pointed to him and said, 'That is for Qing Ming. It is grave-sweeping day. This is when the men are supposed to take care of their ancestors' graves. We must clean them and burn ghost money. But many people are too far from their home towns, especially if they have come from the countryside to the city. So they can only do this, burn some ghost money for their relations. Many of my workers do this because they are from other provinces.'

Da Ming had relocated his family from where his ancestors had lived for generations. The only things he couldn't move were their graves. When I asked if he was going back to Shaoyang for Qing Ming he said, 'No, I don't need to. My uncle lives in Longhui, near Shaoyang. He will go for me.'

In the hotel he'd booked for me I was the only guest. While I was searching for my passport, Da Ming paid the desk clerk. When I protested, he said, 'Don't worry, you are my guest. It is only a little money.' He yawned. 'I am very tired.'

'How much do you normally sleep?'

'Maybe five hours. Sometimes less. Often I must be awake to talk to a customer in America.'

We said goodnight, then he added, 'Tomorrow I will come here at ten. We will go somewhere special.'

I slept, and dreamed of an orchard in which I walked without clothes. I was woken at 7.30 by drilling, followed by banging, shouting, more drilling, then a cry of rage. After this there was silence, till Da Ming banged on my door. We went downstairs and got in the car where his wife and son were waiting.

As he drove Da Ming and I spoke about his old classmates. He also had news of one of my former teaching colleagues, Mr Ma, who was famous for having once been a spy. When I'd left Shaoyang he'd been trying, without success, to find a job elsewhere. The college leaders kept refusing to allow him to leave, and without their permission, he couldn't find a government job.

'He had a very difficult time,' said Da Ming. 'He tried to leave for six years! But in the end he has the success. He is now in Huizhou, in Guangdong province.'

'Why did they let him leave?'

'He paid them. About 50,000 yuan.'

'*That* much?'

Da Ming lifted a hand from the steering wheel, then let it drop. 'It is not so much money.'

'It's 50 times what your workers earn per month.'

He shrugged. 'It is not a lot for many people here.'

I didn't know what to say. I hoped he was just trying to impress me. If not, he'd forgotten very quickly what it was like not to have much money.

We drove in silence till we reached a 20-foot-tall statue of a white tiger by the side of the road. 'Here we are!' announced Da Ming.

My surprise was a day in Chimelong Paradise, the largest amusement park in China. The park contains a variety of rides and shows, seven different roller coasters, a safari park, a circus and 'a world-advanced 4D cinema'. Despite the high cost of admission – tickets to the park and circus cost 320 yuan each, a quarter of one of Da Ming's workers' monthly salaries – the park was crowded with families and young couples. The air was loud with muzak and screams. There were roller coasters with multiple twists, giant pendulums that looked incredibly unsafe, log rides that drenched anyone who came near. In Shaoyang the leisure options had been limited. You could go to the cinema that had only one screen, walk by the river, play mah-jong, sit in the park (where you were fined if you walked on the grass) or sing karaoke. The closest thing to a theme park was a four-hour bus ride away, in Shaoshan, the birthplace of Chairman Mao. There you could visit a museum, eat Mao's favourite dishes in restaurants and see the house he grew up in, complete with the pig pen, 'the place for farm implements', 'the room where He would gather the family for meetings', and 'the room to put the treadle-operated tilt hammer for hulling rice'.

Da Ming and his family were happy. It was the first day they'd spent together in months. I went on the rides and watched the performances, and did not ask about his factory. We saw a lumberjack show where burly American men hacked at logs while mini-skirted blonde girls wiggled their hips. Then, after taking photos in front of a giant purple tower on which plastic white tigers squatted, we watched more Americans competing with each other, this time on motorbikes and jet skis. There were fist fights. There were explosions.

The climax of our outing was a visit to the circus. This began with a gala procession of figures in cartoon outfits, followed by the grand entrance of a blonde young woman in a diaphanous gown. Next came bears on bicycles, then elephants that played football.

When a tank came on stage, its gun pointing at the audience, I heard people gasp. It moved forward, its turret rose; there was a loud bang, followed by smoke. As it cleared, a white flag popped out of the turret. Then the hatch opened and a chimpanzee in an American general's uniform raised its arms in surrender. The man next to me stood, followed by his wife, and then the people around us, till most of the audience was on its feet, cheering, lost in applause. Their enthusiasm was so drainingly total that when afterwards a podium rose from the floor with a roaring white tiger and an almost naked princess, the crowd's reaction was muted. It took the release of a flock of white doves to rouse them again.

We filed out into the warm evening. Da Ming was quick to ask me, 'Was it wonderful?'

'Very,' I said.

We went to a restaurant with large tanks of seafood: not just fish, but lobsters, crabs, turtles, eels and some vicious-looking black prawns. Da Ming offered me the menu. 'Please, help yourself.'

The first ten pages were filled with photos of expensive crustaceans. I had a suspicion that the costlier the dish I ordered, the happier Da Ming would be.

'What about the tofu?' I said. It cost 15 yuan.

Da Ming looked doubtful. 'What about lobster? That is very tasty. You know, I come here often with clients. Sometimes we will spend 1,000 yuan. Nowadays in China this is very common.'

I stood up. 'Do you mind if I look at the tanks? That'll help me choose.'

Da Ming gave me a puzzled look. His wife stared in confusion.

As I performed a slow circuit of the tanks, I caught glimpses of Da Ming and his wife through the bubbles. They seemed to be arguing, and I guessed it had something to do with me. I considered antennae, twine-bound claws, the terrapins' weak necks. Then I went back to the table and said, 'Shall we have some shrimp?' As they were being scooped from the tank, Da Ming's phone rang.

He got up and went outside. His wife and I smiled at each other. I poured her some tea, she said thank you, and then we sat in a silence that soon become awkward. She broke it by asking where I was going next, and I said, 'Huizhou.' She sipped some tea; it seemed the end of the conversation. But then she put the cup down gently and said, 'He is lucky you were his friend. It made his English very good. If you did not talk a lot, he would not be translator, then he would not have this company. He is very grateful.'

It took me a moment to absorb this. Despite having seen how simply they usually lived, it had not occurred to me that all this expense was for my benefit.

After breakfast next morning we drove to the factory, where Da Ming had a meeting.

'But first I will give you a tour.'

We went into a long, low-ceilinged room, most of which was taken up by a workbench where a young woman was cutting a sheet of plastic with a power saw. As she worked, sparks flew into her apron; she was wearing no eye protection. At the far end of the room a thin man was placing fabric under a heavy press. He pressed a button and the press stamped down so loudly I imagined its effect on a hand. When the press rose, he removed the fabric, checked it, then placed another piece of fabric beneath. He did ten of these during the minute I watched him, which meant he probably did four or five hundred an hour, time enough for the mind to wander, a finger to be in the wrong place.

'How long are their shifts?' I asked Da Ming.

He thought for a moment. 'Six hours.'

Upstairs girls were sewing, cutting and gluing, working quickly in silence. The only sounds were the whirr of sewing machines, the occasional fall of a hammer. At the far end of the room a young man sat by himself in a corner, working a foot-powered treadle with such an air of disgrace that the task seemed a punishment.

At another table workers were putting finished mobile phone cases into plastic sleeves with a blue piece of card.

'These are some part-time workers,' said Da Ming and laughed. I was surprised to recognise his father and mother, both of whom said hello without ceasing to work. I watched leather, plastic and vinyl being moulded, cut and stitched.

'Do you actually pay them?'

'No,' he said. 'They just want to help.'

Da Ming's meeting was with one of his suppliers, a small man with bright eyes and a slightly pinched face. The three of us sat in the office and drank tea that had been packed inside an orange for twenty years. It was from Yunnan province, and tasted like orange-flavoured smoke. Da Ming said it had doubled in price, because there was a drought.

They spoke of mobile phones, chargers and prices. I had stopped listening when Da Ming said, in English, 'He is from near Shaoyang. From Loudi.'

Loudi is a three-hour train ride from Shaoyang, which qualifies as 'near' in China. I told Da Ming it seemed a happy coincidence that his supplier came from a place so close to his home town.

'Actually, this is very common. Many of my partners come from places in Hunan. One of my suppliers is from Huaihua. Another is from Zhuzhou.'

'How come?'

'We have more in common. It is easier to trust someone if you know where they're from. If there's a problem, people find out. If we owe each other money, that is OK; it is good business for us to wait until their business is strong again. In my first year he was very patient, and so now I give him some orders.'

Given they were all far from home, these allegiances made sense. I ventured the opinion that this was a good kind of *guanxi*, an idea Da Ming rejected.

'*Guanxi* is corruption. With good friends, you can have good *guanxi*. But friendship must be first.'

There were still several hours before my train. Da Ming asked if I wanted to go for a massage. In the past, with others, I had turned such offers down, as they were usually just a euphemism for going to a brothel. But I decided that couldn't be what Da Ming intended. I was tired of expecting the worst.

We drove to what looked like a small hotel, where women in cyan tunics welcomed us as we entered. They ushered us into a small room with no windows, two reclining chairs and a large TV. We removed our shoes and socks, and leaned back. The women returned with basins of hot water. They began to wash our feet, which felt wonderful and awkward. I asked Da Ming his plans for the future. When he answered, his eyes were closed.

'I will have a bigger factory, then maybe many factories. But I hope I can stop before I am old. Maybe I will go to some place in the country. When I was in college I wrote a lot. I would like to do that again. It is a good dream.'

Then he was asleep. I shut my eyes and focused on the hands moulding my feet. Even when cold lotion was applied, I did not open my eyes, not until I heard the click of a lighter. The woman was heating a small porcelain cup. When she placed it on my foot, it sucked in the flesh.

Da Ming slept for 15 minutes, then woke and looked confused. For a second he didn't seem to recognize me, or perhaps thought I was part of a dream. Then he bent, put on socks and shoes, stood and said, 'Let's go.'

We made one final stop en route to the station. Da Ming went into the bank, then came out several minutes later with a red envelope. He handed it to me and said, 'This is for you. I want you to have a good trip.'

Inside was a large wad of red 100-yuan notes. There looked to be at least 50 of them.

'Thanks very much,' I said, and put the envelope in my pocket.

3

THE MANY TRIALS
OF MR HORSE

From Guangzhou I took a train east to visit my old colleague Mr Ma in Huizhou. Everyone in Shaoyang Teachers' College had known that Mr Ma used to be a spy. If this was supposed to be a secret, it was badly kept. It was also hard to believe. When I first met him, in 1999, Mr Ma was in his mid-thirties and had a frequent look of astonishment. He wore black glasses with thick lenses; his hair was in retreat. He was bashful, polite, prone to excessive laughter. But the fact that he didn't look or act like a spy only made the rumours more plausible.

When Mr Ma first invited me for lunch I had only been teaching in the college a few months. I was already starting to crack from the stress of being the only foreigner in Shaoyang. Whenever I went into town people pointed at me or shouted several words to demonstrate their mastery of English. Usually this was just 'What your name?' or 'Hello!' (the latter pronounced with a mocking slowness), but 'One, two, three!' and 'I love you!' were also in their repertory. I wanted someone to talk to in a normal fashion, and though I had several hundred 19-year-old students who would have gladly listened, it didn't seem appropriate to say to them, 'I think I'm going crazy.' I had hoped to find friends among my fellow teachers, but they showed an impressive degree of perseverance in their steadfast refusal to have much to do with me. Though they said 'Hello' or 'Good morning', our only long conversations involved them asking me to explain gerunds or the subjunctive.

It wasn't that they were unfriendly, more that they were wary. The previous foreign teachers, two young British men, had fallen foul of the college authorities, one by marrying the young teacher who had been assigned to help him, the other by telling the president of the college that he was a stupid old man. The president had tried to stop the wedding by telling the girl's parents that the foreign teacher had many other girlfriends.

Most teachers had been in the college over a decade and would probably stay until they retired. Few had any pedagogic zeal: their default teaching method was to stand on the raised concrete dais behind their desk and read out the textbook, pausing every five minutes to turn and inscribe a word on the blackboard with calligraphic precision. The reason they kept doing a job they didn't like and which paid poorly (half the salary of a post office worker or railway guard) was that it was a stable job that provided accommodation and healthcare, what was known as an 'iron rice bowl'.

Mr Ma and I ate our first meal together in a small restaurant by the college gate. The floor was covered with tissues and chopsticks; a white dog with greasy fur sulked next to a cauldron of rice. We ordered baked aubergine, pork with green chilli, fried tofu and a cabbage soup. 'Some beer?' said Mr Ma, and although I had marking to do, I thought one drink couldn't hurt. While we waited he asked where I was from in England, if I was married, if I had brothers or sisters, how long I planned to stay in China. I asked how long he had been in the college.

'Four years! Do you think it is a long time?'

'Maybe,' I said.

'For me it is. The conditions are not good. Many students are lazy and we must teach some very difficult courses.'

I didn't agree with him about the students, but his job was definitely much harder than mine. The Chinese education system was (and is) based on the model of learning a textbook then replicating its contents in an exam. Most contain cultural and linguistic errors like the ones I found in *Oral English*, the book I was supposed to teach:

Ways to talk about people and things bad:
He is a couch potato.
He is a soure [*sic*] loser.
He is dirt, no better.
He is a cold sort of fish.
She is a blabbermouth.
He is a Yuppie (hippie, punk)
He is a gay.

As a 'foreign expert', I could refuse to use this book (which the college made all the students buy anyway), but Mr Ma and the other teachers had no choice, often with absurd results.

'Sometimes there is a mistake but we must teach it anyway. If the students write the correct answer in the exam, they will not get the mark.' He shook his head. 'It is a big headache. I don't know what to do.'

For a moment he was disconsolate. Then he grinned, pushed his glasses back, and said, 'But if our goose is already cooked we shouldn't worry!' He lifted his plastic cup of warm beer. 'This is a wonderful day, it is the first time we have lunch together. We should say cheers!'

He downed his beer. I did the same. 'Thanks for that!' he said, and refilled our cups. Although the bottle was still half full, he called for another. It was brought with our food, and for the next few minutes all we did was eat. Then Mr Ma said, 'Nick, you can call me "Horse".'

Most of my students had chosen English names, often because they liked the sound of the word. In one class there were 'Adidas', 'Camel' and 'Salon', plus a host of strange neologisms: 'Brogy', 'Bund',

'Clant', 'Serut'. If one of them had said their English name was Horse, I would have believed them, then told them to change it. In Mr Ma's case, I knew it was just because that was what his Chinese surname meant. But I still felt uncomfortable calling an adult man 'Horse'.

'Is that also your English name?' I asked.

'No,' he said. 'It is the name of a famous English writer. Can you guess?'

'I don't think so.'

'Lawrence!'

We finished the bottle, then started another. Mr Ma told me he was from Xin Xiao, a neighbouring county to Shaoyang, where his parents still lived, along with his wife and son. I asked how often he saw them.

'Every two weeks.'

'Is it hard not seeing them more often?'

'No,' he said and looked surprised by the question. 'Shall we have some wine?'

He didn't mean wine made from grapes, but *baijiu*, the 40 per cent proof spirit made from sorghum that tastes awful, turns the face red and burns the throat when vomited.

'Why not?' I said. 'But do you mind if we shift tables and sit outside?'

The sunshine was warm; I had to ask the question.

'What did you do before you came here?'

The question seemed to please him. 'Maybe this will be a little exciting for you, because I was in the army in Shenzhen, near Hong Kong. You could say I was like James Bond!'

'Oh! And how was that?'

'Very good. But it was hard work.'

'In what way?'

'I had to listen to many hours of people on the phone. And there was a lot of waiting. When you watch someone it takes a long time, sometimes all night. I was always tired.'

'What else did you do?'

'Sometimes we blocked the BBC and some other stations by transmitting pop music on their frequencies.'

'I think the BBC are blocked at the moment.'

'Probably,' he said and raised his glass. 'To the BBC. They are better than the Voice of America.'

We drank and talked for a while. Then Mr Ma said, 'Excuse me, Nick, do you mind if I make a call?'

I watched him go to the other side of the street. He was stood next to a vegetable stall whose owner was a smiling old woman with terrible teeth who sold bad tomatoes. She looked at Mr Ma, who was waving his hand in the air while talking, then across the road and saw me. When she held up a tomato I looked away, down the street where students from the nearby junior middle school were swarming down the road. They wore blue and white uniforms with the red scarf of the Young Pioneers. They were headed home or to the internet cafes that had just opened.

When Mr Ma came back he said, 'I hope you don't mind, I have called some friends.'

I don't remember much about that evening. I know his friends were men who wore dark suits or leather jackets. I know we drank a lot. We went to a karaoke bar called T-TAC where I sang so badly people didn't even laugh. I was told that I had insisted on playing Connect 4 with several of the hostesses. And if it was anything like our subsequent nights out, there would have been a point where the alcohol transformed Mr Ma into a figure so zany and fast-talking he resembled Groucho Marx. This usually lasted about an hour before he transformed again, this time into a sullen figure with bleary eyes who chain-smoked and refused to sing. We became good friends, but there was definitely a paranoid phase when I wondered if anyone ever stopped being a spy, if him telling me this was a kind of double bluff meant to conceal the fact that he was going to report anything I said about sensitive topics like Taiwan,

Tibet or the supposedly 'evil cult' of tai chi practitioners known as Falun Gong.

There were two reasons for Mr Ma's unhappiness. One was that he wanted to teach in a university in Huizhou but the leaders in Shaoyang wouldn't release him from his contract. Without their permission, there would be a black mark on his state employment record that would stop him working in any other college or university. This was a problem all the teachers faced, even the dean of the English department, who struggled for several years just to be allowed to take a three-month sabbatical for a course in Beijing. And it wasn't just teachers whose professional lives were controlled. I knew doctors and nurses who were prevented from leaving their hospitals, even for periods of training. This was the problem with the iron rice bowl: it was also a trap.

There were many cogent professional reasons for leaving Shaoyang Teachers' College, not least that the college leaders were more interested in beautifying the campus for visiting dignitaries than improving the classrooms or the students' dormitories, both of which were crowded, had broken windows and were often without power. One of their greatest follies was to decide that one of the teaching buildings needed to have a small moat dug round it, perhaps to give it a kind of fortified grandeur. After this was completed, a baby fell into it and drowned.

But Mr Ma's most acute reason for wanting to leave was more personal. Sometimes when I asked him what he had done at the weekend, he would answer, with limpid eyes, 'I was just alone with my sorrow.' For reasons Mr Ma never made clear (and which I never asked about), his marriage had run out of love. He had been all but separated from his wife for two years, but she wouldn't agree to a divorce. In 2000 the divorce rate in China was only 10 per cent, partly because there were many difficult official requirements (such as gaining permission from one's employer, who also had to approve any marriage), but also because there was still a social stigma attached to being divorced, especially for women.[1]

I only met Mr Ma's wife once, when I went with him to his village for a weekend the following spring. We changed buses three times, and each time the road got smaller, and more neglected, until it was a series of muddy craters that made the driver curse. The village houses were made of wood and yellow ochre-coloured bricks. Among these were a few two- or three-storey concrete houses covered in white tiles, usually the sign of a son or daughter sending money from their job in a city. Mr Ma's parents and wife lived in one of these, supported more by her salary than his. She was a short, quietly spoken woman who worked as a tax official in a nearby town. When I went with her and Mr Ma for lunch, we were unexpectedly joined by six men who insisted on paying for the meal. When I asked Mr Ma who they were, he said, 'They are local businessmen.' When I asked if this might be seen as corruption, he laughed and said, 'This is very normal!'

After many drinks, Mr Ma and I went back to his house and watched a film whose plot consisted of Japanese soldiers committing progressively worse atrocities. An old woman was being pushed down a well when he asked if I wanted to find a girlfriend in Shaoyang. I said I thought it was too complicated.

'What about the students? There are some very beautiful ones.'

'True. But in England you would be fired for doing that.'

He was aghast. 'That is too strict.'

Next morning we walked off our hangovers in the surrounding fields. We found an old stone hut with carvings of birds on its walls, and a lost black puppy whose eyes were still closed. It took half an hour of going from house to house before we found someone who would take it. I asked Mr Ma why the others had said no.

'They thought we were trying to sell it.'

That afternoon we played with his four-year-old son. He was a sweet boy who was repeatedly amazed that I could make a pen disappear into one ear then emerge from the other; on several occasions he had to be stopped from jamming the pen into his ear. At no point during the weekend did I see any signs of rancour between Mr Ma and his wife. There was no ill-feeling; just an absence of love. On the way back to Shaoyang, as the bus bumped through the dark, Mr Ma said, 'It is a great sorrow and I don't know what to do. I try to tell her that sometimes people cannot be together. But every time I say "divorce" she cries.'

Like most people in China, they had married young. There was (and still is) a lot of pressure on men and women to marry before they are 25. This, coupled with the social and legal restrictions on divorce, meant that I knew many other young couples who were unhappy together. Though China was changing fast, with many new opportunities emerging, there were still numerous official constraints on people's professional and personal lives. When I left Shaoyang in 2001, Mr Ma was no closer to finding a solution to either. The only times I saw him properly happy were when he was out drinking, or when he was talking about his life before coming to Shaoyang Teachers' College. Perhaps that was why he spoke so freely about his former career in espionage. It was a reminder of other, better times, a kind of escape.

At my farewell dinner, in a wooden restaurant overlooking the river, I asked friends, teachers and former students to say what they wanted to happen in their future. Most spoke of travelling abroad or getting rich. A few said they wanted China to grow and become more open. Mr Ma was the last to speak. He seemed to be mulling different ideas over, weighing possible futures. Finally, he smiled.

'Bigamy. That would be nice.'

*

Huizhou is 150 kilometres east of Guangzhou and only slightly larger than Shaoyang, but the similarities end there. In Huizhou, there were palm trees and wide boulevards and the buildings were basically mirrors. Most were less than ten years old; only a few shrinking pockets of single-storey houses with sloping roofs suggested the city's previous incarnation. This metamorphosis was the product of the dramatic increase in prosperity that has swept the cities of China's east coast since the 1990s, an economic boom that spread from the Pearl River Delta cities of Guangzhou, Shenzhen and Dongguan, which are clustered round Huizhou.

At the train station, it was easy to find Mr Ma in the crowd. The only change the years had made was to push back his hairline a few inches. He still wore black glasses, but they now had designer frames. He was wearing light-grey trousers and a short-sleeved white shirt, a look of unfussy elegance. As we drove through sun-bleached streets we skipped through the script of reunion. His exclamations of pleasure gave way to questions ('Are you married?', 'Are you taller?'). We left the city centre and passed between high buildings for several minutes till there was no one in sight and it felt as if we were driving out of town. This sensation persisted so long it became implausible, a disquietingly strange feeling of being trapped in a town that is perpetually ending and yet cannot end.

We slowed as we approached a vast, upturned metal conch surrounded by a devastation of earth and scaffolding. The structure had either been exhumed or was due to be buried.

'That will be a swimming pool,' said Mr Ma. 'The steel is excellent.'

We stopped in front of a ten-storey building partially covered in blue mirrored glass. A red banner hanging from its roof proclaimed, 'WELCOME! GUESTS!'

'This is the university hotel,' said Mr Ma. 'It is not finished. But they have a room for you.'

My room had several excellent features. In addition to a mah-jong table, there were two complimentary packs of condoms on the bedside table. One was called 'Duet Fetherlight'; the other was nameless and featured a black-and-white photo of a Caucasian couple embracing and the words 'Woman + Man, Vibrating'. Less welcome was the fact that the bathroom had a wall of strengthened glass that looked directly into the bedroom and made me feel very exposed when in the shower or sitting on the toilet. And then there was the cacophony from the unfinished floors being drilled, scraped, banged and hammered from 8 a.m. to 11 p.m.

We went to a nearby restaurant and ordered too much food. Mr Ma asked if I wanted beer or *baijiu*. When I said 'beer' he looked disappointed.

I asked him how he had finally managed to get the authorities in Shaoyang to release him.

'It was so difficult,' he said. 'I came here and taught for a month in the summer in 2003, and things were very good, but the leaders in Shaoyang made me come back. I did not want to, but I had no choice. And then I had to wait a long time before I could try again.'

'How long?'

'Four years. I came again in 2007, and I taught for a month, and again they brought me back. But when I tried in 2008 they gave me permission.'

'Why? Was there a change in the regulations?'

'No, I just had to pay.'

It cost him 50,000 yuan; his monthly salary was 1,300 yuan. He had to use all his savings and borrow money from friends, but he was finally free. As we walked around the campus that afternoon it was obvious why he had fought so hard to come there. The teaching buildings and apartments were newer and better laid out than in Shaoyang Teachers' College; we could see the hills that rose in the distance. Bushes lined the roads and paths; feral cats slunk in their shade. The classrooms were also better equipped, most with audiovisual facilities, though I was strangely happy to see they still had blackboards. On one of them someone had written 'HE DIED A GLORIOUS DEATH.'

In Shaoyang Mr Ma's flat had been a series of gloomy, sparsely furnished rooms, not so much the home of a bachelor, more that of a fugitive. His new flat was bright and full of heavy, lacquered chairs that seemed made of bone. The walls were covered with landscape paintings and calligraphy scrolls. On the shelves there were framed photos of his parents and his son, but none of his wife. I was wondering how to broach the subject of his marriage when Mr Ma asked me what I was writing about at present. When I said, 'Thomas Pynchon,' he asked who he was and what he had written. As I explained, Mr Ma reached for a book on his desk called *Survey of American Literature*. He looked through the index, turned to a page, then said, 'It says Pynchon wrote a book in 1958 called *A Crime in Berlin*.'

'I don't think he did. Can I see?'

Although I was sure the book was wrong – Pynchon's first book, *The Crying of Lot 49*, was published in 1966 – there was still a giddy moment when I wondered if there was in fact some secret novel by Pynchon known only to Chinese scholars (alas, there isn't).

'Nick, do you know Huizhou's West Lake? It is a famous beautiful place.'

When I said that I did not know it, Mr Ma was very surprised.

'Really? But I think it is well known around the world for its Five Lakes, Six Bridges and Eighteen Interests.'

By the time we made it through the rush-hour traffic, it was approaching dusk. I counted the lakes, the bridges, then asked, 'What are these eighteen interests?'

'I don't know. It is just a saying.' He stared at a woman wearing very tight black trousers. 'But perhaps we can find some interesting things ourselves.'

We sat under a willow and watched swallows skim the lake. We took it in turns to pick things of interest. I started with the Ming-dynasty tower on the island in the centre of the lake. Mr Ma followed by pointing out the dog sniffing around my bottom. He then picked four more interesting things, all of which were women. After I picked a small boy driving a toy tractor with flashing lights and a police siren, Mr Ma countered with monks. They were wearing yellow robes and walking so slowly and smoothly they seemed to be gliding.

'I like this place,' he said. 'In Shaoyang there is nowhere like this. If you go to the river there it is so dirty you cannot relax.'

The tower was built of layered wood and brick, and said to have magical properties. As we approached, Mr Ma told me that on rare occasions there is a haze at the top of the tower, somewhat like smoke, but finer, as if silk is being spun in the air. It has only happened four times in the last sixty years, and is thought by some to signal the appearance of a Buddha.

'But it is just mosquitoes,' he said.

We climbed, pausing twice: once for breath, the second time to enjoy the view. Lights were picking out the roads. The windows of the tallest buildings each contained a fire.

At the top of the tower we found a teenage boy and girl who stopped talking when they saw us. She was crying and staring out over the lake. He stood apart from her, with his arms folded. We immediately went back down.

It was dark as we walked along the lake. I asked Mr Ma about his wife.

'She is still in Xin Xiao, with my son. But we are now separated.'

He said this with neither regret nor satisfaction; I did not ask for more details. In the last decade, the divorce rate in China has doubled from 10 to 20 per cent, mainly due to the withdrawal of the state from many aspects of private life (e.g. one no longer needs the approval of one's employer) and the lessening of the taboo surrounding separation. In some regions, such as Guangdong province, women now initiate the majority of divorces, perhaps because women from rural areas now have more opportunities for financial independence.

We left the lake and walked to a dumpling restaurant, where two of Mr Ma's colleagues were waiting. Jiaying and Meilin were in their late twenties; both spoke English with an American accent. Jiaying spent the meal talking on her mobile phone while shelling sunflower seeds with one hand. We hadn't finished eating when she apologised and said she had to leave because her friend was ill. After she left, Meilin laughed and said, 'Her friend is very sick! I think no doctor can cure him.'

'What's wrong with him?'

'He has the worst disease. It is love.'

She raised her eyebrows and blew out her cheeks as if nothing were more ridiculous. Mr Ma laughed and said, 'Yes, she has a new boyfriend.'

'A new patient!' said Meilin. 'You know, she is my very good friend but I think she is crazy. Now I want us to eat.'

She put a fried dumpling in my bowl, then one in Mr Ma's. As soon as he had picked it up with his chopsticks, she put in another.

'He will get fat, but that is good. It suits a man his age.'

She kept up this teasing in the taxi that took us back to the campus. By the time we arrived, I felt that she and Mr Ma were either already cautiously together in some fashion, or on the verge of being. The last thing she said to him was that she had ordered a new shirt and trousers for him.

'Clothes make the man,' said Mr Ma, to which she replied, 'Yes, good clothes can improve the looks of a mediocre man.'

But she said it fondly.

PART II

4

A TWISTED LOVE

In today's Beijing the Chinese tourists walk in long, happy lines, wearing red or yellow caps, grasping small flags like victors' pennants as they pose for photos. But in the late 1990s most Chinese people had never visited their nation's capital. It was either too far away or they couldn't afford the trip. The only people I knew in Shaoyang who'd been to Beijing were teachers or doctors who'd been sent there for training. Out of my hundreds of students, only one had been, but all were convinced it was an excellent place. Whenever I mentioned having been to Beijing, someone would ask me, 'Was it beautiful?' or 'Was it wonderful?' Their expression suggested there could only be one answer.

This put me in a difficult position, because I didn't think Beijing was either beautiful or wonderful. Yet I didn't want to insult a place they obviously felt proud of, even if their ideas about it had been gleaned from TV programmes that depicted the city as both a storehouse of ancient treasures and a symbol of modernity. What these programmes didn't show were Beijing's grey, polluted skies, the traffic jams, the omnipresent cranes and construction sites, the gargantuan buildings that embellished their utilitarian architecture with temple-like structures placed atop them like crowns. Admittedly, my view of the place was heavily coloured by the fact that I was usually ill when there. When I first came to Beijing, in 1999, the pollution made my throat swell up so much I couldn't speak for days. In 2001 I spent a week in hospital, giving blood samples, having various body parts scanned and answering questions like 'How often do you cry?' or 'Do you ever feel an almost uncontrollable rage?' (I never found out what was wrong with me.)

The Beijing 2008 Olympics elevated the city's profile, boosting both domestic and foreign tourism. Its opening ceremony attracted most praise; the *Sydney Morning Herald* was especially gushing: 'The world may never witness a ceremony of the magnitude and ingenuity as that which opens the 2008 Olympics.'[1]

Five years later Beijing was synonymous with the worst qualities of China's big cities. Clear blue skies have been rare for a long time in Beijing, but by 2012 the city's catastrophic air pollution was being called 'an airpocalypse'[2] and inspired many photo galleries.[3] There were images of people wearing face masks, or even with gas masks in some cases. The skies in the pictures were grey, brown, the colour of dirty water. Buildings several blocks away were only blurs in the haze. Performance artists staged mock ceremonies praying for clean air, face masks were put onto statues and videos of pop songs with lyrics that had been altered to mock Beijing's poor air quickly went viral on the internet.[4] When several phone apps that provided air-quality data became available, downloads of these quickly reached one million.

But while people's eyes and noses told them something was wrong, within China there was confusion about the severity of the problem. One reason was that while both the Chinese government and the World Health Organization use Air Quality Index (AQI) numbers that measure carbon monoxide, nitrogen oxide, sulphur dioxide and two kinds of particulate matter – tiny flecks of soot emitted by factories and internal-combustion engines – they use very different sets of labels (and warnings) to describe the same AQI figures.[5] Pollution levels the World Health Organization describes as a 'significant concern' are described by the Chinese authorities as 'good' air. In official discourse there is far more talk of *wumai* (meaning 'haze') than *wuran* (meaning 'pollution').

There was also disagreement about how much of the pollution came from sources within the city, such as construction, industry, coal burning and motor vehicles (many of which use poor-quality diesel or petrol), or whether it was blowing in from coal-intensive heavy industry from Hebei and other surrounding provinces.[6] The large cities in these provinces had some of the most severe air pollution in the country; in the list of the top ten cities with the worst air pollution, Beijing often didn't appear. The city's geographical conditions were also blamed: like Los Angeles, Beijing is surrounded by mountain ranges that trap pollution, and often sandstorms blow in from the Gobi Desert.

Given the Chinese public's growing concern about the environment – especially food safety – the government had to be seen to be addressing the problem. In 2013 they announced a 100-billion-yuan pollution plan that promised to address air pollution and sewage treatment.[7] But it was obvious there would be no significant improvement in the near future; the World Health Organization predicted that the air in Beijing wouldn't be safe until at least 2030.[8] Some had already concluded that face masks wouldn't be enough. When interviewed by the *Guardian*, a pregnant woman explained why she felt forced to wear a heavy-duty respirator while out and about in Beijing, saying, 'I'm doing the most I can to make sure I breathe clean air, but if you want to stay in this city, you have to endure the environment – there is no way out.'[9]

Residents' exposure to pollution is at least partly determined by their income. Beijing's many air-conditioned shopping malls have become a clean-air haven for the affluent. Some of Beijing's most expensive private schools hold their sporting activities within huge inflatable domes. 'We were finding our sports fixtures were being cancelled so often, and kids were getting cabin fever from being kept indoors so much of the time,' said one teacher at the British

School of Beijing, where the school fees cost £20,000 a year. 'But now we have the dome, it's perfect weather all year round.'[10]

Whatever one's income, staying in the city means risking one's health. In 2015 a study by Beijing University examining air quality in China's provincial capitals concluded that one out of every seven deaths in these cities was because of air pollution, making breathing the air almost as risky as smoking.[11] Another study found that mothers who were pregnant during the brief period of cleaner air just before the 2008 Olympics gave birth to healthier babies than those who were pregnant in 2007 or 2009.[12]

Yet despite the toxic air, property prices remained high. In December 2015, a plot of cleared land in Chaoyang district sold for such a high sum that the cost to the developer of each apartment would likely be more than the asking price. Guo Yi, a director at a property development consulting agency in Beijing, summed up this situation with the Chinese proverb, 'The flour is more expensive than the bread.'[13]

Beijing's pollution also didn't dissuade migrants from other provinces. According to the 2010 census, Beijing had 7 million migrants living there, about 35 per cent of its total population.[14] When I went to Beijing in April 2014 it was partly to try to understand the continued attraction of the place, and also to see if there was anything of its heritage remaining. I confess I was also curious about what it would feel like to breathe such polluted air; whether it might, for example, have a particular taste.

On the day I arrived the Air Quality Index was 178, which was low for Beijing (though higher than most US and European cities, where the average AQI is between 50 and 100). But the sky was still the colour of slate; even the cars on a nine-lane road seemed to have given up moving. I stood outside the metro at Wangfujing, hoping that being a stationary, single foreigner would allow the person I was meeting to identify me. I waited 20 minutes past the time we'd arranged, and then a young man with a sweaty face came up to me.

'Nick?' he said, and I nodded. 'I am so sorry, I have been in hell. I went ten stops being squeezed to death and then I could not get out. I am sorry.'

Fengyan was a third-year marketing student at Beijing's No. 2 Foreign Language Institute. He was originally from Hunan, and had been one of Xiao Long's best students at the senior school. As we descended into the subway he told me his mother was a doctor and his father drove a taxi, a fact Fengyan thought needed elaboration.

'He is sitting down all day. And so my father is fat!' he said, then laughed.

At 21, Fengyan had already made the transition from village to small town, then to the big city, that multiple generations of his family had been unable (or unwilling) to make. Like Wenli, this didn't seem to faze him. Though not as obviously hip as Wenli – his Adidas backpack and Slipknot T-shirt made him look like a high-school student, an impression underlined by his valiant effort at a moustache – I thought he didn't stick out. But he admitted to being self-conscious about his speech, as he still spoke with a Hunan accent. The transition had been tricky in other ways, not least in terms of manners.

'I was wild, so I had to calm down. Sometimes when I ate I would make a noise in my mouth. After I got a warning from my parents, I was worried whenever I ate.'

When we reached the subway platform it was crowded. 'Back into hell,' said Fengyan. After a minute the train arrived and we pushed on, and then more people pushed on behind us.

Fengyan sighed, then said, 'Everyone wants to come to Beijing. I don't know why they do. They can stay in their home towns, or go to some smaller place, and not have to struggle with working so much.'

'Maybe because of an idea,' I said.

'Yes,' he said and made a sound of disgust. 'I wish it wasn't the capital.'

In the crush we lapsed into silence. Through arms, and between heads, I looked down the carriage. Most people's faces looked as weary or blank as those on the London Underground. But there was one difference: almost no one was reading. Instead most people were staring at games or TV programmes on their phones. Over the next few months I would see the same thing all over the country. Fifteen years ago, when I first came to China, people of all ages read magazines, newspapers and books on public transport. It was shocking to think that the habits of literacy could be lost so fast.

'You should get ready,' said Fengyan as the train began to slow. He took several deep breaths, then added, 'It will be a fight.'

The warning didn't prepare me. When the doors opened at Yong An Dong Li station, there were two walls to get through – people on the train blocking the doors and those trying to get on. As I went through the first wall my elbow connected with someone and I heard a sharp intake of breath, then a sound of distress. But there was no time to apologise. The wall of people who'd been on the platform had already filled most of the spaces left by those who'd already got out. There was no way to get off the train without forcing my way through this second wall, which I did, but this left me with a sense of wrongdoing.

We were going to Yong An Dong Li, a small street in Chaoyang district, between the second and third east ring roads. Over the last decade the surrounding area had been radically transformed, mainly by the Jianwai SOHO development, which covers 700,000 square metres and includes office space, residential properties and over 200 stores. SOHO China is the country's largest property developer; its owners, Zhang Xin and her husband Pan Shiyi, ranked 62nd on China's rich list in 2016.[15] They are also possibly the only property tycoons who profess to be of the Bahá'í faith.

But the huge, pink, mirrored arch that dominates Yong An Dong Li wasn't built by SOHO. Though constructed in 2009, it recalls the craze for blue and green reflective windows that raged throughout China in the 1990s. The blame for this kitsch folly lies with Tange Associates, an architectural firm who also built Beijing's Olympic Village. The company was founded by Kenzō Tange, who designed elegant, modernist buildings all over the world, many of them influenced by Le Corbusier. His son, Paul Tange, is now the company's chief executive; on its website he advances the opinion that

> architecture is not only about designing a city or a building, but just as important is the creation of a feel-good environment for the inhabitants. Each newly designed and completed structure must become one with its surroundings and society in general.[16]

If this homily was meant sincerely, then the pink arch must be considered doubly wrong, as it was neither in accord with the SOHO buildings (which did at least look blandly modern) nor with the remnants of Beijing's old neighbourhoods in the area.

It was one of these that Fengyan and I had come to see. A high grey undulating wall marked the boundary of one of central Beijing's few remaining *danwei*, the work units that provided housing, education, healthcare and a social community to state employees. While these had once been the norm for people throughout China, they were now virtually archaic. One could imagine that in a few years' time the experience of living in a *danwei* would become as alien to most young Chinese people as the notion of gathering in a crowd of thousands to brandish a little red book.

The *danwei* we were visiting had been established in the mid-1950s as a printing factory, but this had closed in the mid-1990s. As the *danwei* was state-funded, the employees had been able to continue living there despite the absence of work. The fact that *danwei* were administered by the state also meant the land they were on was outside the jurisdiction of the city authorities, and thus couldn't easily be demolished to make way for new construction.

But given the value of the land, it was inevitable that eventually the *danwei* would have to go. On a long red noticeboard that extolled the virtues of 'PATRIOTISM INNOVATION INCLUSIVENESS VIRTUE', a row of pasted memos announced that residents' apartments were going to be visited by a team of assessors so that the correct amount of compensation could be determined.

Though the *danwei* probably only had between six months and a year before its demolition, inside there was no sense of crisis. The elderly residents moved slowly between the three-storey buildings carrying small bags of shopping or being gently led by small dogs. Pigeons blinked and shifted in rows of wire-meshed coops. A man stood over an oil-stained sheet staring at the strewn parts of a motorcycle engine. Next to him, a boy hit the ground with a plastic hammer that squeaked.

In many ways *danwei* epitomised the Maoist system. They did more than just provide material needs – they were also a method of ideological and social control. *Danwei* mainly administered people's *hukou* – and *hukou* were used for rationing necessities like grain and cooking oil. In addition, each *danwei* also kept a personal file on its members that contained information about their work performance and political attitudes – without it one couldn't transfer to another *danwei* (an obstacle that had kept Mr Ma stuck in Shaoyang for years). But it also gave people a social identity, and was a kind of extended public family. Up until the 1980s, when people met for the first time they would ask each other what *danwei* they belonged to. Someone who wasn't a member of a *danwei* was often viewed with suspicion.

The origins of the *danwei* system, at least in spatial terms, go back a long way – a walled compound has been the basic unit of Chinese cities for several thousand years. *Danwei*, as a social system, can be traced back to the Communist Party's headquarters in Yan'an, in Shaanxi province, from 1936 to 1948, when it was struggling against the Guomindang for control of the country. The *danwei* was also influenced by Soviet collectives and the organisation of guilds and criminal gangs in Republican China in the 1920s.

Though there's a tendency to view every aspect of Communist societies as the result of authoritarian central planning, in the Soviet Union, and later in China, the collective arose somewhat accidentally. In the early Soviet era, apartments were built close to factories to reduce travelling time; in response to food shortages, factories had to open canteens to feed their workers. The result was a semi-closed community where personal relationships were often political (and vice versa).

After the Communists took power in China in 1949, there was little urban planning during the following three decades. This was partly due to the agrarian nature of the movement, and also because of China's demographics at that time – only 10 per cent of the population lived in cities. Mao also didn't want cities to be anything other than centres of industrial development. However, when he reportedly told urban planners, 'It's no good if cities are too big', he wasn't just worried about conventional urban problems. He was also considering the consequences of a nuclear attack by the United States. Such concerns would later lead Mao to order the construction of fallout shelters all over Beijing (although in 1969 it was the Soviet Union that became the perceived threat). The nuclear shelters were apparently capable of holding the city's entire population, 6 million at that time.

The initial *danwei*-like system aimed to provide former workers from the Guomindang regime with material assistance based around their workplace. This was intended as a temporary measure – the government was supposed to introduce national social insurance, but this never happened. Instead this arrangement became the de facto model for the workplace. By 1957, 90 per cent of the urban workforce belonged to a *danwei*.

The central government were responsible for funding *danwei*, and also determined their layout and appearance. In 1955 there was a campaign against waste in construction in both the USSR and China, which led to a reduction in living space, the introduction of shared cooking and washing facilities, and avoidance of any external ornamentation on buildings. The cheap and austere buildings that resulted epitomised one of the political slogans of the time: 'production first, life later' (*xian shengchan, hou shenghuo*). One of the main reasons why so many Chinese cities were (and are) such uninviting places to live is that their centres were primarily industrial. In 1982, 55 per cent of Beijing's factories were in the city centre.

Fengyan and I stopped to ask an old woman wearing blue slippers where she was going to move to. She was so hunched she spoke without looking up. 'I don't know,' she said. 'But they will give us two houses in another place.'

This didn't seem likely, but I hoped it was true. When we asked another woman where she planned to live next, she paused from watering her geraniums to tell us she was going to stay with her sister in Tianjian. 'I don't want to,' she said. 'I've lived here 50 years. My sister has a cat that smells bad. But I don't know anyone else.'

Like several other residents we spoke to, she had first come to the *danwei* in 1958 after her home had been razed to make way for the construction of the Great Hall of the People. But few seemed especially sad or sentimental at the thought of leaving. One man with grey-streaked hair joked about the flurry of renovations people had been making when it was announced that the assessors would be visiting. 'Some people have added five or ten light bulbs to their homes because they think they'll get more compensation.'

'Are they right?'

'I don't know. But it's OK to try.'

Some residents in China have gone much further to improve the amount of compensation they receive. In 2006 the Shanghai municipal government announced that the number of registered residents in a household could be an alternative criterion to floor space when determining payments.[17] The authorities were seeking to hasten the departure of 150 households so that construction on a new office tower in Pudong could begin. What they didn't expect was the sudden increase in divorce rates among these households. People remarried others with children and adult children got married, in some cases boosting household sizes by two or three times. All this was made possible (and perhaps initiated) by marriage brokers, who helped people find new partners.

The decline of the *danwei* system began with Deng Xiaoping's economic reforms in the 1980s.[18] These allowed for private enterprise and thus a whole system of employment, housing and commerce (especially food) that wasn't tied to the state. During the 1980s most urban residents were still part of a *danwei*, and from 1982 to 1986 some workers could even pass their state job to their children when they retired. Some *danwei* adapted to the changing economic environment by converting sections of their perimeter walls into retail spaces they either rented or ran themselves. And though many were eager to risk the vicissitudes of the new labour market, the exodus from the state sector happened cautiously. In many families, there was what became known as 'one family, two systems', whereby one parent kept their state job, even though it didn't pay well, because it provided a degree of security (mainly in terms of housing and healthcare).

By the mid-1990s people were less likely to describe themselves primarily in terms of which work unit they were part of – there was a shift from being a '*danwei* person' (*danwei ren*) to being a 'social person' (*shehui ren*). Some commentators, like the essayist He Xinghan, didn't mourn the work unit's demise, citing the factional struggles, petty rivalries and competition for resources that was part of *danwei* life.

The work unit has always faced obstacles. From birth it was suffused with politics. The daily time-table [*sic*] of the revolution was to prepare the way for the use of traditional notions of love and

77

benevolence so that a new generation of publicly spirited people would develop. Unfortunately for the revolution, what motivates humans to carry out activities is largely the pursuit of their own personal interests [...] Within the unit itself, they attempted to get hold of, or get more out of, the 'big pot' which everyone shared.[19]

For He Xinghan, the *danwei* was so fatally compromised by its members' scramble for resources that it bore comparison with a person who had 'a huge cancerous tumour'.

Another problem with the *danwei* system was that it wasn't providing enough housing. In 1982 almost half of all urban Chinese families had inadequate housing – many married couples had to live in their parents' apartments or separately in work unit dormitories. The country had been too consumed by major upheavals, like the famine of the Great Leap Forward and then the chaos of the Cultural Revolution, to carry out much urban planning, and so little housing had been built. The frenzy of construction that began after the economic reforms (and which still continues) was at least in part due to the shortage of housing in most cities.

In 1994 the government further eroded the barriers between the public and private spheres by giving *danwei* residents the option to buy their own homes, usually at a vastly reduced price. They were also given the right to resell the property after five years. Essentially, the government wanted all housing to be subject to market forces –a parallel, cheaper, state-owned system would only undermine the property market.

Fengyan and I spent another hour wandering around, then went to eat lunch in a small restaurant near the gate. When he rolled up his sleeve before eating I saw a tattoo on his wrist. It was upside down, but in English, and as I tried to read it he noticed. He looked embarrassed, then rotated his arm so I could see it said 'My way'.

'I got it when I was 18,' he said, perhaps by way of explanation. 'If you don't like it, you could get it removed.'

'You shouldn't, it can remind you,' he said, then our food arrived. He didn't make a noise as he ate.

When we went outside, a small group of workmen were sitting in the shade of a tree, eating rice and meat from tin cups. They were middle-aged and had a worn but healthy look about them. They'd come from Shandong province to work on demolishing the *danwei*, but were having to wait for the assessors.

I asked one of them how much longer they thought it would be. He had a cigarette in his mouth, and didn't reply for a second. Then he blew out smoke and said, 'It will be soon.'

His optimism was echoed by the young man in the small, one-room building that served as the residents' information centre. He wore a blue polo shirt and was initially adamant that he wouldn't answer any questions. 'But it's OK if you look around,' he said, which I did, not that there was much to see. Three colourful posters showing gleaming apartment blocks were taped to the walls; on a movable whiteboard in the corner someone had drawn a triangle with a smiley face inside it.

We were about to leave when the man said, 'The plans are very advanced. There will be ten teams coming to make the assessments and make offers to the residents.'

He paused, and then seemed to imagine we had asked another question.

'This is a very important and sensitive matter; we will try and do whatever we can to be fair to the people living here. The government takes this very seriously.'

'Alright,' I said, and then the man smiled, perhaps in relief that I wasn't going to be one of those awkward foreign journalists who treated anything that a Chinese official said with automatic scepticism. We spoke for several more minutes; the man said he liked reading *The Economist* when he could get it. Then there was the sound of slippers shuffling on concrete as an old man entered. He didn't say anything, just came slowly forward, one arm slightly in front of him. In his hand he held two walnuts still in their shells. He was turning them round each other like meditation balls. When I said hello, he turned and only then seemed to notice me. He started speaking in a loud, high voice I couldn't follow, then broke off and came and took my hand with his free hand.

'The Chinese media never says what is really happening,' he said. 'It will be very good if you tell the truth.' Having delivered this edict, he shuffled off. The walnuts kept turning.

*

After leaving Yong An Dong Li, I went to the top of the city's tallest building, the China World Trade Center Tower III (so named for its resemblance to the former Twin Towers in New York). From the restaurant on its 80th floor I looked out over skyscrapers that reached to the horizon. Directly below, another grand arch rose, one so huge and modern-looking it made the Tange Associates arch seem even worse. This one looked like it had been snapped and then badly glued together. Or as if there were some invisible mirror producing a distorted reflection of an arch – a metaphor that at least nods to the building's purpose as headquarters for China Central Television (CCTV), the state-run broadcasting network.

The CCTV tower has been the subject of ridicule – locals call it 'big pants', while one Chinese critic claimed it had been inspired by a sexually explicit photograph of a woman on her knees. But it's only one of the many eccentric buildings that have appeared all over the country, some of which resemble teapots, a violin *and* a piano, or massive striped eggs. Though the Chinese President Xi Jinping has denounced this trend – arguing that buildings should be 'like sunshine from the blue sky and the breeze in spring that will inspire minds, warm hearts, cultivate taste and clean up undesirable work styles'[20] – these weird buildings at least add variation and interest to the generally homogenous character of most large Chinese cities. From that lofty vantage, looking at all the steel and chrome towers, it was hard to imagine that any *danwei* would be around in ten years' time.

I went and got a drink at the bar, where I started talking to a woman in her mid-thirties. She was wearing a simple but probably very expensive white dress; her hair was cut in a pixie style. She said she owned and ran a make-up company that mostly did work for films, and that she had been a make-up artist herself. She asked whether I was in Beijing on holiday or for business, and I tried to explain something of my reasons for being there, how I was trying to understand the changes in the cities, and perhaps in people's minds.

She thought for a moment, then said, 'It has all happened too fast. People have money and cars and a lot of other things, but they do not have culture. Maybe only 15 per cent of people do. The rest only think about money.'

'Is that likely to change?'

'Yes, it will be better. But it will take 25 years.'

*

When I'd first visited Beijing in 1999 it had been easy to find places within central Beijing that still functioned on a human scale. If I walked a few blocks north from Chang'an Road, the long, wide avenue that runs from east to west and passes by Tiananmen Square, the Great Hall of the People, the National Museum and Wangfujing (a shopping area named after a well of sweet water), then the buildings would soon shrink and the streets would become narrow. There I could witness the gentle theatre of communal life that was Beijing's *hutong*, the maze of alleys dating from the Ming dynasty. I saw bicycles being fixed, children kicking balls, birds hopping in wooden cages, old people resting in the shade, slurping tea from jars. Men in vests squatted around card games while flatbed tricycles squeaked past, laden with scrap metal, cardboard, chairs, chickens, watermelons, shoes, anything that could be made to fit, however precariously.

There's a tendency among foreigners to romanticise the *hutong* neighbourhoods, but there were certainly challenges to living in them: most of their courtyard houses lacked sanitation and heating and didn't offer much privacy. But they were one of the last remnants of old Beijing to survive the multiple phases of demolition that swept through the city during the twentieth century. At the end of the nineteenth century Beijing had an elaborate series of fortifications and defences, most of them dating from the fourteenth century. These included outer and inner walls, multiple gates, towers, barbicans and a moat system. The first serious damage to this occurred during the Boxer Rebellion, when almost all the different imperial nations involved managed to destroy a gate tower or section of wall, usually with cannons. In 1901 British troops tore down an eastern part of the outer wall so a railway line could enter the inner city. After the Qing dynasty collapsed in 1911, the new republican government dismantled more of the walls, or cut arches for trains to pass through. But there were also political motives for the destruction of these and other urban structures. As early as 1912 a newspaper editorial was complaining about the 'great political reformers' keen to tear down everything that was old because it was thereby associated with the imperial regime.[21]

When the Communists took control of Beijing in 1949, they too wanted to reshape the city. Though there were suggestions, most notably by the architect Liang Sicheng, that additional archways could allow the walls to be preserved, the city's outer and inner walls were dismantled during the 1950s. Liang also advocated building a new administrative centre outside the centre of Beijing, a plan that was rejected. Though this was a sound idea, the political climate was wrong: it wasn't until July 2015, when central Beijing's air pollution had reached toxic levels, that the government announced that many of its departments would be moving to the Tongzhou district in the east of the city.[22]

The remnants of Beijing's walls and fortifications were further reduced by the construction of Beijing's subway in the mid-1960s. The only trace of the city gates that were destroyed is in the names of some stops on lines 1 and 2 of Beijing's metro system, such as Dongzhimen, Jianguomen and Chaoyangmen ('Men' means gate in Chinese).

The chaos of the Cultural Revolution – when temples were smashed, books burnt and anything old was a target for fury – further reduced Beijing's tangible heritage. By the end of the 1970s, the *hutong* were one of the city's greatest surviving cultural assets, and not just in physical terms. In these neighbourhoods the bonds of community often spanned generations, allowing local history and culture to be preserved. Some idea of the tightness and stability of these communities can be gained from the fact that the police chief of Jiaodoukou, a neighbourhood to the north-west of Tiananmen Square, used to periodically test his officers' knowledge of the area by grabbing the register of households, calling out a name, and asking where that person lived.

But the long-established communities of Beijing's *hutong* were no safer from the wrecking ball. In 1949 there were 6,074 *hutong*; by 2005 there would be only 1,571.[23] While the State Bureau of Cultural Relics had designated them as protected areas, the fines for their demolition were paltry compared to the profits that could be gained through property development in these neighbourhoods.

The dwindling of old Beijing wasn't unopposed. As early as the mid-1990s doubts were being expressed about the effects of the city's rapid growth on its culture and quality of life. The writer Chen Jiangong spoke of it becoming 'a city where it's impossible to find a spot to hang up one's birdcage'.[24] In Qiu Huadong's 1997 novel *City Tank* there's a visceral disgust for the changes: Beijing at night is compared to 'a huge cancerous stomach ulcer floating amidst the lights'.[25]

Wang Xiaoshuai's 2001 film, *Beijing Bicycle*, provides an invaluable record of some of these neighbourhoods while also showing some of the changes that were taking place within them. The film tells the story of two boys: Jian, from a low-income family, who wants a bicycle to impress a girl, and Guei, who has come from the countryside to be a bicycle messenger in the city. Though Jian manages to buy a bicycle second hand, it turns out to be stolen from Guei. The conflict over the bike eventually becomes violent. The film subtly shows the two boys' different but equally potent aspirations: Jian is desperate for social status, while Guei wants to leave behind his rural origins, yet the irony is that their desperate desire for a bicycle only further identifies them both as outsiders. In the first three decades of Communist rule, people's material aspirations were summarised by the phrase *sanshengyixiang* – which referred to owning a bicycle, wristwatch and sewing machine.[26] By the 2000s many urban Chinese had their sights on much more ambitious goals, like owning a car or their own home.

Watching *Beijing Bicycle* today it's hard to believe this was the Beijing of only 15 years ago. The iconic flocks of bicycles have mostly gone – today, only 12 per cent of commuters in Beijing pedal to work, compared with 38 per cent in 2000.[27] But the biggest difference is the physical landscape. The pace of demolition in the city increased during the 2000s. According to UNESCO, between 2003 and 2006 a third of the 62 km^2 area that made up the central part of the old city was destroyed, displacing around 580,000 people.[28] Much of this was in preparation for the 2008 Olympics. While this was a source of pride for many Chinese people, the relentless destruction of homes had a human cost. In September 2003 one resident burnt himself to death while being forcibly evicted; another attempted suicide by jumping off a bridge to oppose destruction of his home.[29] Attempts to provide legal protection for these tenants were either ignored or dealt with harshly: one activist who sought to protect tenants' rights was charged with revealing state secrets.[30] After this, many lawyers were afraid to take on such cases. This intimidation of legal activists still persists. In November 2015, the housing rights activists Jia Lingmin and Liu Diwei were given prison sentences in Zhengzhou, Henan for 'picking quarrels and provoking troubles', a blanket charge often used against activists.[31]

But some people continue to fight for Beijing's architectural and cultural history. He Shuzhong is head of the Beijing Cultural Heritage Protection Center (CHP), an NGO that has the quixotic task of trying to protect the country's architectural history.[32] We met in a Starbucks that at the time seemed only averagely noisy – the hum of people, the grind and hiss of the coffee machine – but when I came to transcribe the interview it sounded like we'd been in a helicopter. Mr He's short hair was greying at the temples; although it was the weekend he was smartly dressed in a black sports jacket. He looked serious but without seeming stern; over the course of the hour we spent talking he often laughed or smiled wryly.

Mr He credits the origin of his interest in conservation to when he was an intern at the Shanghai History Museum while he was a college student.[33] He saw that the museum was chronically under-staffed and unable to stop many works being lost or damaged; theft and sale of antiquities on the black market was particularly rife in China in the 1990s. He wrote an article decrying this trend, which generated a lot of positive responses and encouraged him to keep promoting heritage preservation. In 1998, when working as a law professor in Beijing, he launched a small group, staffed by volunteers, called Cultural Heritage Watch; in 2003 this was renamed and formally recognised as an NGO, a far from straightforward process in China (many of them aren't really NGOs – the fact that they often need a government sponsor means they are better thought of as GONGOs: government-owned non-government organisations, a contradiction in terms).

Not all of the CHP's work has taken place in Beijing – in the mid- to late 2000s, its volunteers worked in Sichuan and Yunnan provinces to document different aspects of local culture, both tangible and intangible. However, since then, the majority of the organisation's efforts have gone into trying to protect Beijing's historic neighbourhoods. According to Mr He, while the government was willing to spend a lot of money on restoring the Summer Palace and other famous sites, anything that fell outside of this narrowly defined idea of 'cultural heritage' received no protection: 'For most Chinese people a museum means a new, large building. An old village or a *hutong* means "poor" and undeveloped. They think these places are dirty and terrible!'

In Mr He's opinion, the problem was due to the swiftness with which China's economy has grown: 'Ten years' development happens in one year in China, a century's worth in ten years. And this is very bad, but this is the reality. Since 1949, there have been two periods: in the first one people only cared about politics; in the second they only care about making money. Because of this experience, people do not understand the cultural heritage. They don't respect the cultural heritage. So they need help to understand. The cultural heritage doesn't belong to the Communist Party – it belongs to each person. So each person should protect the cultural heritage.'

The CHP uses lectures and meetings to teach people about local history. Having educated and mobilised a community, which takes multiple meetings, they then approach the media to gain publicity and support. To date, their greatest success has been saving the Gulou residential areas. These are spread around Beijing's Drum Tower (which for many centuries was used to signal the time), just to the north of the Forbidden City. When it was announced in early 2010 that the area would be demolished to make way for an underground museum, many Beijingers were aghast: these were some of the best-preserved *hutong* in the city. Mr He said that the meetings organised by the CHP had attracted a lot of attention. 'At the last one, 2,000 people came and the local officials told us we must cancel it. We said, "You cancel the plan, and we will the cancel the meeting. There are cultural protection laws in China. We are not fighting against you – we are only for the law."'

In September 2010 the demolition was cancelled, which set an important precedent for the role of citizen activism in cultural preservation. But Mr He was quick to acknowledge that gaining widespread support for a preservation campaign sometimes isn't enough. Generally, most development schemes cannot be stopped. Often the best hope is to limit the damage caused by the development.

In their highest-profile campaign to date they went up against SOHO China, who in 2007 planned to demolish and rebuild the Qianmen area located to the south of Tiananmen Square. Qianmen is the geographical centre of the city – originally it was the front gateway connecting the inner and outer imperial cities. For over 600 years it had been the site of the Dazhalan (literally 'big fence') market; its maze of alleys of small shops and houses was a hub for small traders and migrants. Mr He said that when the CHP obtained the development plans, they started campaigning, but there was an immediate problem: 'The local residents accepted the proposal; why, we didn't know. They also made the local media accept it, because some of the newspapers carried their advertising. We tried our best, but we couldn't do anything, so they started demolishing.'

However, Mr He and his colleagues managed to show that the plans contravened local conservation laws, and, more importantly, were able to attract international support for their campaign. Their tactic, according to Mr He, was more subtle than simply eliciting foreign condemnation, something that has had little effect on Chinese domestic policy (most notably in its treatment of ethnic minorities in Tibet and Xinjiang): 'We addressed the investors in the project. We said the plan is illegal, which means the project is illegal, so your money is unsafe. So the SOHO shares went down. This did not stop the plan. But it had to change.'

In the end, the scale of development was reduced to the main street, which was turned into a pedestrian thoroughfare with shops built in a 1920s style – though the fact that these included chains like H&M and Häagen-Dazs is indicative of the planners' sense of historical authenticity.

Work on other projects in the area stopped at the end of 2008, though SOHO disputed that this was primarily due to conservation concerns.[34] Instead they argued that the problem was a regulation that hampered investment from foreign companies (the company is registered in the Cayman Islands). Nonetheless, the SOHO development still profoundly altered the character of the Qianmen area. At a meeting in 2010 Mr He was quoted as saying that the development was 'a prime example of cultural heritage damage. This area has lost its spirit and soul.'[35]

But when he spoke to me of the campaign, four years later, it was with obvious pride: 'For half a year we struggled, and many small developers watched it on TV. It was a lesson for them.'

I asked him whether the government's continuing urbanisation drive was going to make it harder to protect urban heritage.

He laughed ruefully. 'In this environment, it's almost impossible. However, we must try. Not only for heritage, but for the local people. But as more people crowd into the cities, cultural relics will be destroyed. The important thing is to raise awareness enough to stop things getting worse. Since we can't stop urbanisation, we can try to make it more reasonable.'

Some urban planners and property developers have come to view the 'culture' of an area as a commodity that can enhance its economic value. I asked Mr He whether he thought that might soon be the case in China.

He shook his head. 'That can only happen if they even understand the concept of heritage. Instead they just see a poor and dirty place that is like the Third World. It is the same for many officials. They think "We need to be a leader!" They ask, "Why is this area so quiet? So dark? Why is the road so narrow? Beijing should be a world city!" If someone has a lot of money and power but isn't educated, this is the most terrible combination.'

*

In July 2014 the Chinese government began to clarify some of the ways in which the *hukou* system would be amended.[36] While in theory migrants would be able to apply for permanent residency in any urban centre, in practice there was a daunting set of requirements that would exclude them from gaining residency in China's largest cities. The exception was at the level of the smallest towns (less than half a million people), where migrants would only need to prove they had stable accommodation in order to shift their *hukou*. At the next level up, in cities of between half a million and a million people, the restrictions were tighter – in addition to accommodation and a stable job, they would need to have paid into a local social security fund for a long period of time.

But for medium and larger cities (which includes most provincial capitals in China) the requirements were prohibitive, and involved a points-based system that rewarded people holding college degrees or those who had studied abroad. The catch was that there would be a quota, which meant that even someone like Fengyan, who was going to graduate from a very good university, stood little chance of permanently transferring his *hukou* to Beijing. The *Global Times*, a state-owned newspaper, characterised the competition for *hukou* in Beijing as being like 'thousands of horses and soldiers trying to cross a single log bridge'.[37] On the black market, Beijing *hukou* were said to be selling for around 450,000 yuan (around $75,000). The main tactic was for an agent to find a company or institution that had a quota of *hukou* for their employees, which would then pretend to hire the person. After getting their Beijing *hukou*, the person would leave the company.

Ultimately, the final say about *hukou* criteria was supposed to remain with individual cities – for example, how long an applicant needed to have resided in the city or paid into a local social security fund. But the State Council, China's chief administrative body, did offer some directives. Cities wouldn't be allowed to consider the price or area of an applicant's apartment, and no more than five years' worth of payments to a social-insurance scheme would be necessary (previously, some places had required ten or even 15 years of contributions).

Though the proposed changes were cautious, they still represented a major shift in official discourse. This isn't to say that the topic has been entirely taboo – as far back as 1993, China's State Council had proposed a gradual reform of migration rules and ultimately the abolition of the rural/urban *hukou* distinction.[38] This was followed by a pilot scheme in 1997 in 328 small cities and towns that enabled anyone with a rural *hukou* to switch to being an urban resident, provided they had a stable income and had been living there more than two years. Just over half a million people took advantage of this offer, and there were signs the government meant to expand the scheme. In 2001 the *People's Daily*, usually a good barometer of the Party's intentions, blamed the *hukou* system for widening the urban/rural gap and promoting corruption. In August 2001, the *Chinese Youth Daily* prophesied that 'the cities will become truly filled with energy and hope' only when the 'artificial barriers' of the *hukou* system were removed.[39]

But when the scheme was widened, it quickly became apparent that most cities couldn't afford so many new residents. In Fenghua, Zhejiang province, in just eight months from 2001 to 2002, 13,000 people were granted urban *hukou*, which resulted in a loss of 20 million yuan to the city (the money it would have gained from the additional school fees that rural *hukou* holders would have had to pay). Faced with this potential financial crisis, plans to introduce greater *hukou* reform were quickly shelved. In 2010 the idea of major *hukou* reform was still such a sensitive issue that when 13 newspapers published a joint editorial advocating reform, it was quickly removed by the state and some of the editors were fired.[40]

But even the strictest *hukou* restrictions, such as those in Beijing, aren't intended to stop migrants from coming to big cities to find work; the point is to make sure they don't stay permanently. Any migrant worker whose dream is to bring their whole family to live with them in a major city like Beijing or Shanghai is likely to be disappointed. Without a local *hukou*, there's usually no access to public healthcare or education.

Migrants who do bring their children to live with them in the city thus face the problem of where to send them to school. Though by law all children are entitled to a state education until they turn 16, many urban schools claim they have no places available when migrants apply, mainly because they receive no funding for children without a local *hukou*. Children who can't find a place in a public school have no option but to go to private schools, which have lower standards, higher teacher turnover and are more expensive. Unsurprisingly, some migrant children fall through the crack between public and private education: in Shanghai and Guangzhou, around 5 per cent of migrant children don't attend school at all.[41] The semi-legal status of many private schools also means they have often been targeted by city authorities. In the summer of 2011, 24 of these schools were demolished in Beijing alone;[42] similar destruction occurred in Shanghai and other cities. Some pupils only found out about the closure of their school when they turned up for class at the start of the new term and found the school buildings reduced to rubble.

Even children whose parents have the money or *guanxi* to get them a state school place still face major disadvantages. For example, the textbooks in their new school are often different from those in their home towns. This would be a problem in any country, but in

China, where secondary education is a long, slow struggle to rote learn textbooks for the *gaokao* college entrance exams, such a shift in materials can be disastrous. What further compounds the problem is that the *gaokao* can usually only be taken in their place of *hukou* registration, where the curriculum is often different. Migrant children in public schools often face discrimination and, much like their parents, are generally treated as outsiders, despite the fact that many are 'rural' in name only, having grown up in the city. These children are more comfortable in an urban setting and have little knowledge of country life. It's arguable that these children, who are administratively 'rural' yet 'urban' in most other ways, have most to gain from the proposed changes in the *hukou* system.

The central government and most local authorities have been slow to offer support for migrant education: there was little official recognition it was even an issue until the mid-1990s. In 2002 the Ministry of Education suggested that the government and public schools 'should play a key role in safeguarding the education of migrant children', but the response to this varied greatly between cities.[43] Shanghai was one of the most receptive: by 2009 most public schools in the city were accepting migrant children.

Much of the work done to help migrant pupils is done by NGOs, who raise funds for migrant schools and promote awareness of migrant pupils' difficulties. On a warm Sunday afternoon in April 2014 Fengyan and I went to an event held by Share the Care, an organisation set up by a group of corporate executives in 2010 to help vulnerable children. In previous years, the charity had held sponsored walks, but that year the event was a series of friendly football matches. Most of the teams were sponsored by corporations whose employees paid to take part, but one of the teams was made up of retired players from Beijing Guoan, a famous local team Fengyan had grown up idolising.

The football pitches were at a sports complex far from the centre, and it took over an hour, and several buses, to get there. Apart from the six teams taking part, few other people were present. Without the long stage whose backdrop was emblazoned with the logos of Sony, Nokia, Shell, Intel and Volvo, it could have been a weekend match in the park. Fengyan was too awestruck to speak to any of his heroes, but he did manage some excellent loitering in their close vicinity. He had a front-row seat for their warm-up routine. This consisted of them joking with each other, swallowing sports drinks, rummaging in the glossy gift bags from the sponsors and conducting loud phone conversations, activities they occasionally interrupted to slowly jog to the edge of the penalty box, fire a shot at goal, then saunter back to the rest of their team, in most cases accompanied by jeers or commiserations depending on how wide their shot had been. They all had the calm insouciance of people who were once so excellent at something that they would never have anything else to prove. Meanwhile, on the other pitches, the executives – who were generally a decade younger than the former professionals, and in better shape – ran up and down as if their careers depended on it.

The only other people taking the occasion seriously were two representatives of a property development company who wore identical khaki trousers and white polo shirts. They were handing out colour brochures printed on thick card that advertised a gated development on the edge of the 5th Ring Road. At the time this didn't seem strange – wherever I went in China there were posters and leaflets showing idealised apartment complexes, with the square footage costs printed in hysterically large type. Later, it occurred to me that having property developers at the event was somewhat ironic – property speculation is one of the main reasons why living in Beijing is so unaffordable for many migrants.

The event began with a blare of pop music. A woman in a cream dress boomed a greeting no one returned, and then a line of children from migrant schools shuffled on to the stage. They were wearing school tracksuits or cheap clothing; they kept their eyes on the ground. Each was presented with a tennis racket, then urged to stare at the waiting cameras. Having served their purpose, the children were quickly ushered offstage. They formed a column to one side, and stood in silence while the announcer thanked a long list of sponsors, praised the companies taking part and asked for a special round of applause for the players of Beijing Guoan. While there was nothing objectionable about acknowledging these people, there was a conspicuous failure to mention, let alone discuss, the issue of migrant education. Like the children themselves – who would play no further part in proceedings – it seemed an afterthought.

The matches lasted half an hour and were played in a competitive, though good-humoured manner. Beijing Guoan dominated their opponents, and were winning 3–0 by the middle of the second half. At this point the opposition dared to take advantage of a defensive error and scored an excellent goal. I don't know if the Beijing players regarded this as impertinent, but in the remaining eight minutes they scored three more goals.

Afterwards, on the bus back to the centre, I asked Fengyan what he thought of the event. He looked up from his phone and said, 'It was all propaganda. But I'm glad I saw my heroes.'

This was my last night in Beijing, so we went to eat dumplings. After too much food, I asked Fengyan whether he really wanted to stay in the city, considering how difficult it would be to find a job, let alone get a *hukou*. Given how much he seemed to dislike the crowds and the horrors of public transport, I thought I knew what his answer would be. Yet although he had been scathing about everyone coming to Beijing because it was the capital, and because they believed it might make them, or their children, rich, happy and successful, he too had a kind of faith in the possibilities of the place.

'Yes, I want to stay here, even though it will be hard. You know, there are many things I don't like about Beijing, and sometimes I hate it. But I don't want anyone not from here to say bad things about this city. It's a twisted love.'

5

LEFT BEHIND

In June 2015 four children died in a village in Guizhou province after drinking pesticide. The youngest was five, the oldest thirteen. It wasn't an accident. The eldest child left a note to his parents that said, 'Thanks for your good intentions. I know you are good to me, but it is time for me to go. I swore I would not live beyond 15 years old and death has been my dream for years.'[1] The children had been living alone for several years, as their parents had jobs in other provinces. At the time, their mother had been working in a toy factory in Guangdong. When she returned to the village for their cremation she said, 'I have truly failed them.'[2]

The suicides sparked a debate within China about the situation of children left behind in the countryside while their parents work in distant cities. 'Why does [the government] only pay attention to this problem when terrible things like this happen?' one person wrote on Weibo, China's version of Twitter. In mostly rural provinces like Guizhou, between 40 and 50 per cent of children grow up mostly without their parents, as the high level of poverty in these provinces often forces adults to travel far to find work. According to the All-China Women's Federation, there are currently 61 million 'left-behind' children – nationally, about one in five – and their numbers have been going up steeply since 2010. Some of these children have little or no contact with their parents for most of the year, not even by telephone. One NGO found that 15 per cent of the children they surveyed went a whole year without seeing their parents. About 25 per cent received only one phone call every three months.[3]

When I was teaching in Shaoyang it didn't occur to me that many of my students had been left-behind children. Though some were withdrawn and clearly unhappy, there were many other possible causes of misery that seemed more immediate, not least the tedious routines of college life. It wasn't until I knew them better that I realised some had barely seen their parents for years. Many of their English diaries chronicled New Year family reunions that began in joyful fashion, then after a week became melancholy or angry, either from accumulated resentment or because the return of one (or both) of their parents brought bad news. One of my best students wrote in her English diary about finding out that her father had been having an affair with a woman in the city where he'd been working.

20 February

I gave a call to my mother this evening and she told me something bad about my father. I was not surprised but rather angry with him. I don't know what can I do to save him, to save my family. I really don't know what to do. I feel tired, too tired. If I can choose, I'd like to go to a quiet remote place for a whole life.

22 February

I was very sad today, sad for my parents, my sisters, my brothers and my friends too. Do I have the need to live on the earth? I don't know how to face them if I still live. Really, I want to die, thus nothing can hurt me.

27 February

Haven't heard from father for almost 3 weeks, just now he rang me and asked if everything went well with me. I had mixtured [sic] feelings. I love my father. He is a man with ability and he has suffered

a lot for us. On the other hand, I hate him, he has brought so much
trouble to my family, to my mother.

Though most left-behind children live with their relatives, some
have no adult supervision. Such children are especially prone to
accidents: in 2012, five homeless boys died from carbon monoxide
poisoning in the city of Bijie, in Guizhou province.[4] They had started
a fire in a rubbish container in an effort to keep warm.

The plight of left-behind children reflects the widening gap
between cities and the countryside in China. While the country's
economic development since the late 1970s has been remarkable, the
benefits haven't been equally shared. Deng Xiaoping, the architect
of much of China's economic reforms, warned in the early 1980s
that China would remain unstable until the lives of its rural citizens improved. This warning was borne out by frequent protests
by farmers throughout the 1990s, most of them in response to
land seizures, local corruption and onerous taxation. In the 2000s
the state eased farmers' burdens by abolishing most agricultural
taxes and creating free junior school education and cheap medical
insurance, but the income gap between countryside and city today
remains just as large. Guizhou is one of the poorest provinces in
China, at least partly because its mountainous geography means the
roads are poor and there's little good land for agriculture. While the
'Chinese Dream' isn't about making everyone rich, it is nonetheless a
vision of a society where everyone is at least moderately prosperous,
something that seems far off in Guizhou and many other provinces.

Xi Jinping's visit to Guizhou (though not Bijie) in 2015, ten days
after the suicides, was meant to demonstrate that the government
wasn't neglecting rural poverty. Xi was quoted as saying, 'A good
life is created with one's own hands, so poverty is nothing to fear.
If we have determination and confidence, we can overcome any
difficulty.'[5] Such optimistic platitudes are a staple of the Chinese
leadership, but within the state media less confident opinions were

also expressed. The English-language newspaper *China Daily* quoted Tang Jun, a researcher on social policy at the Chinese Academy of Social Sciences, as saying that the suicides 'showed that the government intervention measures have failed. The role of parents cannot be replaced, and the best way is to ensure that the children go with their parents as they migrate to other cities to work.'[6]

In Tang's opinion, the problem was that the *hukou* system relegated migrants to the status of second-class citizens. He argued that for decades China has 'merely required a workforce from the migrant workers. If we do not provide them with more social benefits, similar cases will take place again and again.'[7]

This grim prediction was confirmed several months later, when two children were murdered in a village near Bijie. Zhang Yunyu, a 15-year-old girl, and her 12-year-old brother Zhang Yunhai, were found stabbed to death in their home. They had been staying with their older sister while their father worked elsewhere as a stonemason.[8]

Left-behind children are also more vulnerable to bullying at school; many worry about their own and their parents' safety. One study found that 70 per cent of left-behind children showed signs of anxiety and depression. Without parental care, these children are also more likely to become targets for sexual predators. In April 2014, a 30-year-old teacher in Guizhou was found to have raped 12 young girls, 11 of whom were left-behind children.[9]

The absence of their parents makes many rural children passive and withdrawn; some take advantage of the lack of adult supervision and commit crimes. One study found that 80 per cent of migrant workers with criminal records had been left-behind children.[10] Though most crimes committed by these children tend to be minor offences, like vandalism or theft, some incidents have raised serious questions about what effect the lack of parental care is having on some children's sense of morality. In October 2015 three students, aged between 11 and 13, killed a 52-year-old teacher in Shaodong county in Hunan.[11] The teacher had seen them stealing food from the school shop, and in order to stop her reporting the theft, the boys chased her into a toilet, hit her on the head, then choked her to death. Afterwards they stole her phone and money and went to an internet café.

But while such terrible events make for dramatic headlines, the most common problem among left-behind children is poor school performance. Rural secondary education has high dropout rates, either because the students fail the exam to get into senior school or because a family may be unable (or unwilling) to pay school fees and other costs (primary and junior secondary education is free).[12] In 1990 only 7 per cent of rural children went on to senior middle school – 25 years later it's estimated that only a third do. The high dropout rate means there's little social mobility between generations; on a national level, it translates into a shortage of skilled workers, which China needs if it's going to build a 'moderately prosperous' society.

Increasingly, children are following their absent parents' example and leaving school to go to cities to find work. In a bitter irony, they often end up doing exactly the kind of unskilled, low-paid jobs their parents have been doing to pay for their upbringing. In the 2009 documentary *Last Train Home*, Qin, the daughter of two migrant workers, leaves school and gets a job in a bar in Guangzhou, in what seems both an act of independence and an expression of resentment against her parents. The result is that the family disintegrates – Qin's father's disappointment and anger with his daughter builds until he erupts and hits her.

Qin's story illustrates how many migrant workers' aspirations for their children are thwarted both by economic necessities and the shortcomings of the Chinese educational system. In some ways left-behind children are the mirror images of the urban 'little emperors', the generation of pampered only children who have grown up in China's big cities (the one-child policy only applied to urban regions, one of the few instances where an urban *hukou* was a disadvantage). The lives of (some) people in Beijing or Shanghai might inspire optimism about China's progress towards general prosperity, but conditions in its poorer provinces are arguably a better test.

*

Hunan isn't as poor as Guizhou – it has good agriculture and reasonable infrastructure – yet it still lags behind the coastal provinces. In 2014 Hunan was 17th out of 31 regions by GDP per capita; Guizhou was in last place. When I returned to Shaoyang and other cities in Hunan in 2010, I found they hadn't changed much since I left a decade ago. The low property values in these towns meant there hadn't been a great financial incentive to demolish as much as possible and then build taller, higher-capacity buildings. As a result, the streets were still a palimpsest of different architectural styles: a few high-rise buildings from the 2000s, a lot of four- or five-storey buildings covered with white tiles and mirrored windows from the 1990s, the odd brick factory and warehouse from the 1960s and 1970s, and even some wooden or stone buildings that were older than this.

There were other indicators that Shaoyang and other smaller cities in Hunan were falling behind. My informal, completely unscientific system was to walk the streets and see how long it took for someone to stare at me, or better yet, point out that I was a foreigner. In 1999 this was something that sometimes still happened even in Beijing, but ten years later the majority of people in provincial capitals, and most large cities, had seen enough foreigners, both random and resident, to know there was nothing inherently interesting about them. But in Shaoyang in 2010 it hadn't taken long for a group of schoolgirls to unleash a volley of giggles, then a middle-aged woman to take a sharp breath. It was a kind of homecoming.

In 2014, when I went back to Hunan, the first place I visited was Leiyang, a small city of just over a million people where a friend of mine, Weiping, was teaching in a middle school. Leiyang is a minor city in the orbit of Hengyang, the second-biggest city in the province. Its main claim to fame is being the birthplace of Cai Lun, who is generally credited with inventing paper (as opposed to papyrus). Cai was born in the middle of the first century AD, and was castrated and became a court eunuch in AD 75. He was later placed in charge of making instruments and weapons, suggesting he had a particular technical aptitude. Strictly speaking, Cai didn't invent paper; others had made it previously in China. What he did was improve and standardise the product, mainly by adding other substances to the manufacturing process. This achievement can be credited to his technical ability, to which one can add the appealing legend of Cai having a bolt of inspiration while watching paper wasps make their nests. Today Leiyang is still a centre of paper production.

Weiping's school was in an old complex of buildings near the river. He'd agreed to introduce me to some of his 'left-behind' students in exchange for helping them practise their English. There were three boys and three girls, all of them in senior middle school (i.e. aged between 16 and 18). When we met, they had the typical eagerness to talk that was confounded by a layer of shyness. But there was none of the incredulity at my presence that Xiao Long's rural students had shown in 2010. Though these were 'left-behind' children, they were still urbane.

We took a bus to one of Leiyang's least obvious parks, hidden within the grounds of the Datang Power Plant. At the gates a giant billboard depicted, with incredible chutzpah, a digitally altered photo of the view in front of us. The power station's blue and white Lego-style blocks were faithfully rendered, as were its twin candy-striped towers. But in the happy world of the billboard they weren't belching grey smoke over the city. Instead they rose brightly in a clear, untroubled sky. And just for good measure, the lily of deception had been gilded – the power station had been placed on the crest of a wooded hill.

In the park we walked between stands of bamboo, then climbed the spiral steps of a concrete tower. At the top there were benches and a view over the roofs of apartment blocks. We sat and drank water. I realised I had no idea how to broach the subject of their parents' absence, and wasn't sure I should try. None of the students seemed unhappy or withdrawn – they were eating melon seeds and chatting among themselves – but it still seemed insensitive to ask how they felt about being virtually abandoned. In the end Weiping had to prompt me. He cleared his throat and said, 'Nick would like to ask you some questions about your families.'

They looked at me quizzically. 'What do you want to know?' said Li Lin, a short girl with her hair pulled back into a tight ponytail. She wore blue jeans and a white T-shirt from which a pink tiger stared. On the lapel of her jacket a small British flag attested to the bewildering longevity of the Cool Britannia brand.

'Mine are in Guangdong,' she said. 'I was with them, but I had to come back for the exam.'

Apart from Li Lin, only one of the others had ever been to visit their parents where they worked. Liu Bei said she'd once been to see her father in Dongguan, a factory town in Guangdong, but wouldn't go again. She tugged at her long hair and said, 'It wasn't a good place. It was very boring and my father was too busy to spend time with me. But he has to be there because there are no jobs in our home town.'

The other students agreed with this, but as we talked it became apparent that there were big differences in how the children handled being apart from their parents. Two of the boys claimed not to even know where their parents were working. Before I could ask them any more questions, Weiping said quietly, 'They do know. But they are ashamed.'

The third boy, Xiaotong, wore a neon-pink sweatshirt and had vicious acne. He said he preferred having his parents live far away. 'It's no problem,' he said. Xiaotong lived with his younger sister in a small apartment his parents paid for. 'I look after her, but she is very good. And I am very responsible.'

'He is the father!' said Li Lin, then laughed.

'Or the mother,' said one of the other boys.

Xiaotong may have been putting a brave face on the situation, pretending to prefer a situation he could not control. But although many left-behind children find their parents' absence distressing, it would be a mistake to think that they all feel this way – let alone are suicidal. A 2006 report by the Hunan Youth League found that around 10 per cent of such children didn't miss their parents at all. According to the head of the League: 'Ever since birth, they have been cared for by their grandparents. Some don't even remember what their parents look like. For some left-behind children, the concept of parents is merely symbolic, not a genuinely emotional concept.'[13]

We spent the rest of the afternoon in the park, then I took the students for dinner. I told them to order their favourite dishes, and while we waited for the food I asked what they wanted to do when they left school. Xiaotong said he wanted to start a business; Liu Bei wanted to be a teacher.

Li Lin's dream was to become a designer. 'I make paper flowers,' she said, and brought her hands together. 'Like this,' she said and opened them slowly, her palms unfolding like petals.

*

Leiyang didn't seem like the future. Most of its buildings were shabby, white-tiled structures from the 1990s; many of the shops were glorified garages, concrete boxes with cement floors and roll-down shutters. By the roadside there were vegetable plots and on some of the roundabouts old gravestones stuck up from among cabbages. Some of Leiyang's citizens also had a reactionary approach to dealing with foreigners. It had been a long time since strangers had yelled at me in broken English from the other side of the street. In the lift in my hotel a drunk young man asked, in much better English, 'What is your name?' and then laughed over my reply.

But despite its unprepossessing appearance, Leiyang is an essential part of the Chinese government's urbanisation plan. It's these small- and medium-sized cities, not places like Beijing, that are supposed to grow to accommodate 250 million people over the next few decades. Rather than trying to expand existing megacities (i.e. places with more than 10 million residents), the idea is to develop their surrounding urban centres. The largest city is supposed to act as a hub that will specialise in administration and finance. From it, smaller cities will spread out like the spokes of a wheel. These are intended to have more specialised economies – such as in technology or industry – while being tightly connected to the largest city.[14] This cluster model of urban development is intended to reduce pollution, congestion and resource demand, and thus be more sustainable. The most prominent future cluster is centred around Beijing, the port of Tianjin, and the wider Hebei region. This is intended to become a metropolitan area six times the size of New York's, and home to 130 million.

However, while it's comparatively easy to change the household registration system to allow people with rural *hukou* to settle in cities, the hard part is developing places like Leiyang enough to make this feasible. People need jobs and places to live, and most of all, they have to want to go there. It's one thing to get state-owned banks and businesses to move to a new district of the same city (as happened with Pudong in Shanghai), but reorganising an entire region is another matter, especially since the private sector in China is much stronger than it was in the 1980s, and may resist relocation (though this may not be as great a problem as it at first appears – the line between public and private ownership in China is often blurred).

The key to making the cluster model work is likely to be transportation. Small towns and cities in inner China have generally not been well connected. Getting to Shaoyang from Changsha, the provincial capital, used to require either a four-and-a-half-hour bus ride, a six-hour train ride, or a five-hour drive on bad roads. The same was true for Leiyang until 2009, when its high-speed train station, Leiyang West, became operational. With this, Leiyang became a stop on the Wuhan–Guangzhou rail line, which at the time was the fastest train in the world, with a top speed of around 300 kilometres per hour. This reduced the trip between these two major cities from ten hours to around three and a half, and though some criticised it for being too expensive, every time I took the train its carriages were almost full.

Public confidence in high-speed trains was severely damaged in 2011, when the Minister of Railways was dismissed for corruption and abuse of power. Later that year, two high-speed trains collided in Wenzhou, killing 40 people.[15] The investigation into the crash revealed systemic failures of management and regulation. Though the state tried to suppress media coverage of the incident, there was still widespread public anger. It took several years to restore public confidence, during which the maximum train speed was reduced and the Ministry of Railways was abolished (its duties were absorbed into other departments). Yet by 2014 the high-speed rail network was looking like a plausible way to connect regions that had previously seemed distant from each other into a viable economic whole.[16] Both state and private companies continued investing heavily in rail infrastructure, with 820 billion yuan spent in 2015 alone. In tandem with this, many new airports are also under construction. Though Leiyang isn't due to get one, nearby Hengyang Nanyue Airport, in the south of the city, started offering flights to Beijing, Shanghai and Xi'an in 2014.

Despite the grand plans for Leiyang, it was still hard to imagine the city as a pulsing, vital part of an economic cluster. It wasn't just the crops growing by the road or the Soviet-era apartment buildings; whichever way I walked, the city ended abruptly in fields. In many places this border was marked by courtyard houses built of old grey brick. They had wooden window frames and thick beams supporting high roofs. On their walls the ghosts of old political slogans were fading into the brick. But although there were no people in sight, and no sounds of life, the courtyards were well swept. In one compound an old temple had stubs of incense in jars and a weather-worn banner depicting mythological figures. In another an old woman was lining up *baijiu* bottles along a wall. Before I could speak to her she disappeared into a house.

I stepped through an old stone gateway into a courtyard where shirts and underwear hung from overhead beams. A young woman wearing a black jacket and trousers was washing a bra in a plastic bowl on the ground. When she saw me she stood quickly, called someone's name, and then a door opened. A man poked his head out, then came out smiling, a little surprised but not dismayed. He was holding a half-smoked cigarette, and offered me one, which for many Chinese men is still a ritualised form of greeting. Xiaomao lived with his wife and daughter, whom he supported through growing vegetables and doing manual labour. He'd been born in an adjacent house, where his mother still lived. Xiaomao knocked on her door, and she came out and said, 'Who's this?' She was about four and a half feet tall, wore a shiny pink jacket and black trousers, and had thin wisps of hair combed over her scalp. I told her I was visiting Leiyang and wanted to know how long she'd been living in the house.

'I grew up in a village near here, but when I married my husband we moved to this place. Then it was all fields.' She gestured at the house. 'Many boys were born in that little room,' she said. It sounded like a boast.

'Me and my two brothers were,' said Xiaomao. 'They are in Changsha.'

'Are you married?' she asked me, and when I said no, she shook her head. 'You should hurry up. One of my sons is 36 and single. It's a very big worry.'

Xiaomao's daughter brought us wooden stools to sit on, then he said, 'Leiyang is a very red place. Many people come to visit because of this.'

Xiaomao was referring to Leiyang's role in the birth of the Chinese Communist Party, something true of many places in Hunan, especially Shaoshan, the village where Mao Zedong was born.

'We have produced two generals,' said Xiaomao proudly. 'Do you know Zhu De? He was the first commander of the People's Liberation Army.'

I wondered whether Xiaomao didn't know, or didn't mind, that Zhu De's forces had destroyed most of Leiyang in 1928. This was during the Civil War, when the Communist guerrilla forces were fighting in Hunan. According to a report Mao wrote in July 1928, the region was so ravaged that Zhu's army 'could keep alive only by selling opium'.[17] Zhu's rationale for destroying people's homes was that it would leave the peasants with no choice but to join the Communist uprising. Then, as now, you might argue that the Communist Party was quick to sacrifice ordinary people's welfare to some grand plan for the nation.

Xiaomao's family home had already been selected for demolition, but he wasn't upset about having to move. 'We will get compensation and a free flat,' he said. 'And we will get 600 yuan a month as well. It is a very good thing.'

'What about you?' I asked his mother. 'Will you miss living here?' She shook her head.

*

In Shaoyang there were more elaborate fantasies. From banners and posters the slogan rang out: 'Construct a civilised city – build a beautiful and happy Shaoyang!' And for those whose imaginations were lacking, a glimpse of the future was supplied. At bus stops and on noticeboards a panoramic view of the new Shaoyang was on display. The new, civilised city was going to be the product of careful urban planning. In the distance there were gleaming skyscrapers, in the middle ground more modest apartment buildings, while in the foreground a huge park full of trees ran along the edge of the Shao River. To the right of the park a giant white pyramid of uncertain function emphasised the new Shaoyang's modernity; to the left an official-looking grand red building invoked the nation's past. And like the picture of Leiyang's power plant, existing parts of the city were still present. Two of Shaoyang's three bridges would have a place in the new city, as would the river, though its colour would be improved from milky green to a placid sky blue (the dragon sleeping in it would obviously have to go).

There was, however, no sign in the picture of the city's oldest buildings, its North and East towers, built during the Ming dynasty. These were octagonal and built of yellowish-grey brick; that they didn't merit inclusion in the vision of the future wasn't surprising. I often felt a pinch of disbelief they'd survived as long as they had. Whenever I went back to Shaoyang I made a point of visiting at least one of the towers, just to check they were still there. At the base of the East Tower there was a house where the caretaker lived with his son, who used to drive a motorcycle taxi until a regula-tion was passed banning them from the city for being hazardous and causing congestion. The last time I saw the son he'd been sitting in front of the tower with one of his trouser legs rolled up, slapping his knee repeatedly. He was hitting it very hard, and the knee was swollen and red. 'I'm moving the poison around,' he said. 'Look here.'

I saw a darker patch of skin.

'In Chinese traditional medicine there are sensitive points, and this is one of them. My father does this, and he has no black marks.'

He went back to slapping, then held out his hand.

'Smell this; it's the way that dead people smell.'

He thrust his hand under my nose. I couldn't smell anything.

The new traffic regulations were part of a broader campaign to clean up both the city and its image. Even in the late 1990s, when Chinese society was far less environmentally conscious than it is today, people complained about Shaoyang being dirty. The visit of a minor official could provoke a flurry of street sweeping, but at other times there was no attempt to stop people burning rubbish or throwing it in the river. In 2012 the city tried to address the problem by authorising retirees (in China, often a euphemism for people made redundant) to give out on-the-spot fines for spitting, littering and traffic violations.[18] Shaoyang's Urban Management Bureau gave the inspectors red armbands to identify themselves and let them keep 80 per cent of the fines. There were soon reports of overzealous ticketing, with residents complaining of being ambushed by multiple inspectors when stopped in traffic. The head of the Urban Management Bureau defended the policy by saying that the city was 'trying to improve the urban traffic situation without expending too many of the city's resources'. This may also have been an attempt to reduce the high unemployment in the city – Shaoyang still hasn't recovered from the closure of many state-owned factories in the 1990s. Discontent among the jobless is a major concern for the authorities; there have been several violent incidents involving disgruntled employees. In August 2012, for example, an 'early retiree' from a water company in Shaoyang killed three managers in an arson attack, apparently because they did not hire one of her children.[19]

For the first few hours after I arrived in Shaoyang in May 2014 it was easy to scoff at the dream of the new city. In the centre the shops were still concrete caves, while overhead there was such a confusion of telephone wires it seemed like a method for snaring birds. But Shaoyang's better infrastructure had caused property prices to rise, meaning there was finally money to be made from building new housing. When I walked up the hill from the river I found a street that looked like it had been bombed. The ground was littered with crushed brick and fragments of tile; huge chunks of masonry and twisted metal lined either side of the street. Walking further, I came to an almost empty area the size of several football fields, where earth, bricks and rubble had been piled at the edges, turning the space into an arena of sorts. This effect was heightened by the two 20-storey apartment buildings higher up the slope, both of them nearing completion. But the destruction wasn't absolute. In the centre of the cleared space two small, crooked houses had survived. The demolition of the surrounding streets had left their roofs uneven and their walls missing bricks. Next to them a staircase ended in mid-air, while a stone doorway led nowhere. It reminded me of photos of the Blitz in London that showed entire streets destroyed save for a single building, what must have seemed an almost miraculous reprieve.

In China the sight of these solitary buildings in the midst of destruction has become commonplace. These are known as 'nail houses' on account of the way they stick out, especially when developers remove all the surrounding earth, leaving them elevated and exposed. There are many reasons why the occupants refuse to leave their homes, not least sentimental attachment, but in many cases compensation is a major issue.

Unsurprisingly, some tenants haven't been as trusting as Xiaomao's family in Leiyang, and have taken measures to protect themselves from eviction. The most spectacular example of this happened in Hubei province in 2010, when Yang Youde, a farmer, constructed a makeshift rocket launcher he used to fire warning shots at developers.[20] Yang became a cult figure and was eventually awarded generous compensation. While Yang's actions might seem excessive, some property developers have resorted to threats, kidnapping and arson.[21] Even without these measures, water and electricity are usually cut off in an attempt to get residents to leave.

While Yang became a celebrated figure, most nail households are depicted in unflattering terms. Residents are accused of being motivated solely by greed – one colourful epithet for them describes them as 'tigers blocking the road of progress' (lanluhu). In 2009 an official in Hebei province told a 66-year-old villager who was threatening to jump off a building to protest against the destruction of his home that he should go 'straight to the top floor. Don't choose the first or second.'[22]

There's even been a lack of official sympathy for people who protest more tragically. In September 2010, three people in Yihuang county in Jiangxi province set fire to themselves in protest at the demolition of their homes to make way for a new bus station. While a local official later admitted that their case had been mishandled, he defended the principle of forced demolition, arguing that

everyone is actually a beneficiary of such policies. Without forced demolition, there is no urbanization in China; and without urbanization, there is no brand-new Chinese society. As a result, we can say that without demolition, there would be no new China.[23]

This was 'people-centred' urbanisation.

But the construction crew working on the site in Shaoyang expressed no rancour towards the tenants in the nail house. 'They've been there two years,' said the foreman. 'They don't own it, they are just renting it, but they still want compensation.' He shrugged, perhaps because it wasn't his problem.

I went to the house to speak to the residents, but no one seemed to be home. Through the windows, I could see several rooms had been emptied. The largest room, which had bars on its window, was piled high with a confusion of boxes, clothes, bulging bags and furniture.

'Are they still there?' asked an elderly woman carrying a basket of leeks. When I said yes, she laughed.

'They have no hope. They should have gone last year. We're going to move up there,' she said and pointed to the apartments above. 'It will be cleaner and better.'

She nodded in a satisfied manner. But the residents of the nail house weren't the only ones unhappy with the construction. At the edge of the demolition area there was a skeleton of charred roof timbers; only the side gate of the house was intact. The gate contained several painted panels; from one an orange phoenix peered through smoke damage.

I asked a passing man with grey-streaked hair what had happened. He hesitated, then said, 'Some think it was an accident, but most of us think it was deliberate. The property development company hired some hooligans who set the fire. If they can't use white ways, they will use black ways as well. Before this, the people's windows and doors were broken several times when they were out.'

'Did the police investigate?'

'They did nothing. They are on the side of the developers.'

I asked him where his own house was.

'It has also been pulled down. Now I live outside this area.'

He wasn't the only one who found the fire suspicious. A retired teacher further up the street told me that there had been three such fires since the property developers announced the project. 'And after a fire, they even dared to offer a lower amount of compensation!'

The teacher had his own reasons to be unhappy with the company. He was standing in front of his two-storey house, whose walls were marked with the *chai* character that signals a building's looming demolition. He had signed a contract with the company, and was going to move soon.

'I didn't want to leave. My family has lived here more than 50 years, my father, and my grandfather too. But I can do nothing. I can't stop this city changing.'

6

CUTTING GRASS AND WOOD

In 1979 80 per cent of China's population still lived in the country-side; by 2010 this proportion had halved. Of all the convulsions that have shaken Chinese society in the last 100 years, the shift towards becoming a primarily urban society has arguably been the most revolutionary. Though the countryside witnessed huge upheavals during the Maoist era, first with collectivisation and then with the great famine that followed, neither of these led to the removal of almost an entire generation from rural communities. But the great rush towards the factory towns of Guangdong province has removed the majority of people of working age from the country-side. In many villages, the only people left are grandparents and their grandchildren.

When I lived in Shaoyang, my favourite thing had been to visit my students in the Hunan countryside. The journey alone was an adventure, as it usually involved taking a bus to a small market town I'd barely heard of, then another bus to an even smaller place I'd never heard of, and then having to find a motorbike taxi to take me to the village itself. Given that few people in China had a mobile phone at that point, I couldn't just call if I had a problem – such as when I got on the wrong bus, or had a motorbike taxi driver who said he knew where we were going but then after ten minutes of driving through fields, as dusk approached, admitted he had no idea.

I wanted to see how the continuing exodus to the cities had affected rural life in Hunan, so when Weiping asked if I wanted to accompany him on a trip to his village I was very pleased. But when I asked if he was looking forward to going home, he immediately shook his head. The problem wasn't the three-hour trip to the village in southern Hunan where he'd grown up, or the cost of getting there. He didn't earn a lot of money as a senior middle-school teacher, and apart from wanting the most up-to-date iPhone, he didn't have expensive tastes. It also wasn't because he didn't get on with his family; he said he often missed them. What made going home difficult was the gifts – the money he had to hand out to his relatives.

The gift-giving began before we even got to Weiping's village. On the way, we had to stop and see his grandmother. We got off the bus at a junction on the brow of a small hill, then followed a narrow path that descended in slow curves towards a group of houses clustered around a pond. It had just been raining; as we walked, the flooded fields reflected the sky's shift from grey to blue. Several lines of ducklings watched us. Distantly, dogs barked.

When we arrived, Weiping's grandmother was pumping water into a wooden bucket. She wore a light-pink sweatshirt and grey trousers and had a wrinkled, shiny face. When she saw her grandson, her mouth split into a smile that exposed two silver front teeth. Although Weiping hadn't told her I was coming, she didn't seem fazed. There was also a surprise for Weiping: his aunt came out of the house, wiping her hands on a towel, followed by two boys and a girl. Weiping seemed happy to see the children, but there was something muted about the way he greeted his aunt. She lived in a nearby house with the children, though one of the boys, Xueyou, was her sister's son. His mother was working in Guangzhou; according to Weiping, she called her son once a month.

Xueyou was 16, but looked much younger. He was wearing a pink T-shirt on which 'Style Fashion' was printed in big letters, above which was printed in smaller type 'Cklvin CK alien'. Perhaps to make sure the T-shirt was really 'style fashion', the designers had added one of the 'Angry Birds' from the popular online game of the same name.

Weiping's grandmother asked if I was hungry. 'There's duck,' she said and pointed into the bucket, in which the plucked bird didn't look angry, just dead. While she prepared lunch, Weiping showed me round the house. The kitchen was the largest room, most of which was taken up by an L-shaped iron stove. In the next room there was only a wooden table, some stools, and an altar to their ancestors. His grandmother slept in an adjacent room in a four-poster canopy bed made of dark, heavy wood that was decorated with brightly coloured paintings of tigers and flowers. It had been part of her dowry.

Before we ate, Weiping gave his grandmother 300 yuan (around $45). She hadn't asked him for money but may have expected it, because she only said a simple thank you. As she went to put away the money, Weiping said, 'They live simply, but they need help because there are no jobs here. And she has always been very kind to me.'

For lunch there was duck, cabbage and small eels the children had caught in the rice fields at night. When offered these, I politely declined. 'I'm afraid of them,' I half-joked.

'Me too,' said Xueyou. 'I just like catching them.' He went and got a tree branch that had nails hammered into one end. 'This is what I use,' he said, and mimed the act of impalement.

'It's good for frogs as well,' he added. 'The big ones taste best.'

'But the government has banned us from eating them,' said Weiping's grandmother as she stood and went to the stove. She brought back a pan of rice, scooped some into our bowls, then looked at it distrustfully. 'I'm sorry, it isn't very good,' she said. 'It's been cooked too long.'

After eating a few mouthfuls she pushed away her bowl, then reached under the table and brought up a bottle of rice wine. She poured some into a tin mug, then drank it in two swallows.

'I have this every day,' she said. 'It's very good for my health.'

Weiping's aunt hadn't said much, until this point, but once we'd stopped eating the rice she started asking him questions. She wanted to know about his work, how his girlfriend was, if they had set a date to get married. He answered politely but without saying much. The atmosphere began to seem strained, so to lighten the mood (and because I also had drunk a fair amount of wine), I suggested we all take photos together. Xueyou and the other kids ran outside, but Weiping's aunt asked us to wait. 'There's too much here,' she said and put her hand on her stomach. She went to put on a girdle.

While we waited, Xueyou and the other children kicked a football around. Weiping pointed at him and said, 'His mother had several abortions before he was born, all of which were girls. He's clever, but his scores are average except in maths. The conditions in the school are bad, and there is no one to help at home. It is a pity.'

His aunt came out patting her now reduced stomach. I took photos of her, the children, Weiping and his grandmother in almost every possible combination, then it was time to go, or at least I thought it was. Weiping's aunt said something to him I didn't hear; he nodded without looking at her. She went inside and he followed, then came out a few minutes later.

'We can go now,' he said.

'What was that about?'

He twisted his mouth to the side. 'She wanted money too.'

'Did you give her any?'

'Yes, but not a lot. She is my aunt so I must give her something, but she does not need it. I will need a lot of money soon for my wedding and an apartment, but she does not think about this. And when I get home more people will ask.'

We climbed back to the road, then flagged down a minibus packed with schoolchildren. The children were from Weiping's village but went to school in other districts. Many rural authorities struggle to fund education, and have found it more cost-effective to close schools. A recent report by the Chinese NGO Growing Home said that over the past decade 37,000 schools in rural areas have closed.[1] The withdrawal of public services and the migration of people of working age to the cities have caused many rural communities to dwindle. In 2000 there were 3.6 million villages in China; by 2012 there were only 2.7 million.[2]

The road rose, offering a view of gently terraced fields, some of them flooded, some orange with churned earth. Here and there a stick figure raised a hoe or slowly bent to plant. We crossed an old bridge with revolutionary slogans on its sides, then stopped in a small market town. The main street was lined with fruit stalls and food carts with cracked glass panes, offering cold noodles, fried tofu smeared with chilli, and various parts of pigs. The bricks of the buildings were the same colour as the earth in the fields; rows of wooden houses lined a street that sloped to the river. I had a moment of what seemed like déjà vu, before I realised it was a memory. It was the way parts of Shaoyang had looked when I first arrived.

From the town it was a half-hour walk to the village. On the way we passed Weiping's old primary school, which had closed several years before. Its playground was overgrown with weeds; the concrete ping-pong tables were covered in moss. He walked to a small podium at the front of the playground, then mounted its two steps.

'I used to give speeches to the other students from here. Mostly about patriotic or political things. I was very serious then.'

Above us a door opened, then a man called out. We went up the steps to the first floor and found him living in one of the old classrooms. The others were full of chickens.

It was a hot day, so after 20 minutes we stopped to rest on the edge of a reservoir. A man looked up from a long wooden boat moored nearby, then returned his gaze to the water. At the far end of the reservoir, the ground rose into verdant hills whose slopes were thickly wooded. Dragonflies hummed, and the scene was peaceful, though there were electricity pylons to counteract this timeless rural scene.

From there it was only a short walk by the side of a fast stream until we reached the village. The houses were scattered in small clusters on the higher ground surrounding the fields. Most were two-storey red-brick buildings with grey roof slates and a flat concrete area in front. There were also newer houses, three storeys high, covered in pale-coloured tiles. A few were only concrete shells without doors or windows; Weiping said their families were waiting for the money to complete them. It's been estimated that on average migrants send about a third of their income home to their families, which results in about 10 per cent more money per person in rural households. This has been especially important as the income gap between the city and the countryside has continued to widen – the average rural resident's income is about three times less than that of an urban dweller. Remittances from migrant workers have certainly helped alleviate poverty in most parts of China. However, in some of the poorest regions migration often isn't a viable option. Many don't have the necessary skills or education to find non-agricultural work, and in places where farming conditions are difficult, people often need to stay to work the land. There also may not be enough money to cover the expenses of looking for a job, such as transportation, accommodation and food.

Migration to the cities thus isn't a panacea for all the ills of the countryside. There also need to be enough people left to work in agriculture, and enough non-urban land for them to cultivate. Without this, China won't be able to meet its targets for food self-sufficiency and will become more dependent on food imports.

One reason incomes are so low in the countryside is that agriculture in China has shifted away from small-scale family farms to agribusiness.[3] Most farmers can't compete with large-scale factory farms, and in some cases (such as soybeans and maize) are also unable to match those of imported commodities. Imported

118

soybeans now account for three-quarters of the soybeans made into cooking oil and animal feed in China. Another area in which Chinese rural households have suffered is pork production. When I visited people's homes in the Hunan countryside in the early 2000s it was common to see households keeping a small number of pigs. Raising swine was an easy way for farmers to generate income – one of my students who needed extra money once sighed and said, 'Now my mother will have to get ten more pigs.' But despite rising demand for meat in China, fewer farmers are now bothering to raise pigs, because they can't compete with factory farms. In 1985, 90 per cent of pigs in China were being raised on small farms; by 2007 this was down to 20 per cent.

Weiping's father wasn't home when we arrived, so we sat outside and watched people working in the fields. Near to a small herd of black goats a man wearing a surgical face mask was carefully spraying the crops. 'Watch out,' shouted an elderly woman from an upper window of the house next door, and the man in the face mask raised his hand in acknowledgement.

'The goat owners don't like the farmers using pesticides,' said Weiping. 'They say it makes the goats get sick. But everyone uses them.'

Weiping's elderly neighbour came outside to say hello to him, and then started asking me questions about America. Eventually I told her I was from England.

'But you look American,' she answered, then started speaking to Weiping in a Hunanese dialect I couldn't follow. He made non-committal noises for a few moments, then said in English, 'Let's go inside.'

He shut the door. 'She's so bossy. She says I should buy a chicken from her because you are a guest. She says if I don't you will not feel welcome.'

It was an old house, but the walls had been recently painted and the floor was smoothly tiled. There were two bedrooms, one with a canopy bed, another with a double bed, and a third room that had a table, stools and a well-kept altar to the family's ancestors. Long strips of red paper with prayers painted on them in big black characters framed a shrine bristling with incense. It was a simple but comfortable house; all it lacked was plumbing. The house had a supply of bottled water – the river water wasn't drinkable – but if we wanted to cook or go to the toilet, we had to visit Weiping's grandfather. He lived nearby in a three-room wooden house that was one of the oldest buildings in the village. The main room had a rough stone floor and the air inside was smoky. Sacks and bags hung from hooks in the ceiling. The hearth was black with soot.

His grandfather was frying lumps of pork fat with vegetables when we entered. He looked healthy for 90, except for black patches of skin on his face and a large dark-brown patch behind his ear. He'd grown up in the house, as had his father and grandfather before him.

He asked where I was from, and nodded at the answer. I asked if he'd seen a foreigner before.

'Only on TV. I have a map of the world, but I can't read, so I don't know where England is.'

We ate quietly in the gloom with the door half-open to let the smoke escape. I asked Weiping's grandfather what he thought of conditions in the village.

'So many young people have left to find work. There are now only 40 people left here out of 200. It's only the old taking care of the young. But times are good now. In the 1950s I just had rice and wild vegetables to eat, and during the three bitter years, it was even worse.'

He was referring to the years of famine between 1959 and 1961, when around 40 million starved to death as a result of drought, bad weather and, most of all, government policy. Mao was determined to impose the collectivisation of farming onto the countryside at any cost; local officials exaggerated the grain yields so much that most of the harvest was sent away from the regions that had produced it. Even when millions were dying from starvation, grain was still exported. Yet Weiping's grandfather didn't blame Mao for this.

'He was a great man. He sacrificed his family for the country. His son died in North Korea.'

'What about his mistakes?' I asked, which wasn't an especially contentious question: since Mao's death in 1976, the official position has been that overall Mao was only 70 per cent right.

But Weiping's grandfather didn't put much stock in this view. 'Who doesn't make mistakes?' he said.

There's been a growing forgiveness (or forgetting) in China of Mao's catastrophic errors. On the 120th anniversary of Mao's birth in 2013 the *Global Times* newspaper carried an editorial that argued 'The mistakes that he made [...] cannot be wholly imputed to Mao alone. The responsibility should be taken by the entire nation.'[4] On an everyday level, there are still posters of Mao up in most middle-school classrooms, while in taxis it's common to see a pendant with Mao's face hanging from the rear-view mirror like a protective deity. A local businessman in Henan took things further by erecting a 120-foot golden statue of Mao in early 2016, despite Henan being where the famine was worst.[5] This, however, was an act of worship too far – the statue produced so much online mockery that it was swiftly torn down by the local authorities.

The resurgence of the cult of Mao isn't that surprising – there's never been a free discussion in China of his legacy, and it's unlikely there will be while the Communist Party is in power. Mao can also be co-opted into the narrative of the Chinese Dream being a process of national rejuvenation that he began in 1949 (never mind that Mao opposed mass urbanisation and certainly would have been against the creation of a consumer society). There's also plenty of official hagiography. Liu Jianwu, the dean of the Mao Zedong Research Centre, explained the building of the golden Mao statue by saying, 'In the hearts of ordinary people, Mao represents fairness and justice. So people hold these kinds of emotions towards him.'[6]

After we'd finished eating, Weiping gave his grandfather three crisp red 100-yuan notes, each bearing Mao's face. I used the toilet – which was two planks positioned over a hole – then we climbed the hill behind the house and went looking for Weiping's father. He had fields in three different places; we tried the water-melon patch first. He wasn't there, so we went to the next field, balancing on the narrow paths between irrigation ditches. We didn't find him there either, so we walked another five minutes and found him ploughing a field with a bull. He stopped and came over. Weiping introduced us and I went to shake his hand, but he held it back.

'It's dirty,' he said, and smiled. Although this was true, his hand was also shaking badly. Later Weiping told me that the doctors didn't know the cause of the tremors.

Weiping asked his father if he needed help.

'Can you cut some grass for the bull?' he said. 'You know the place.'

We went back to the watermelon field, and spent a long time trying to find the sickle. Eventually we found it tucked under a patch of clover-like leaves; they were thickly dusted with a white insecticide powder that made them look diseased. Weiping started cutting the grass while I collected lengths of straw to tie it into bush-els. He cut quickly and skilfully; I'd only just managed to badly tie one bushel – it came undone as soon as I picked up the bundle – by the time he'd finished.

'It's OK,' he said, and knelt by the pile of grass. In less than a minute he tied the rest of the grass into three bundles. It was just a small demonstration of competence, but it signified how easily he could switch from being a teacher living in a modern apartment in a city to being the child who'd grown up helping on the farm.

It was dusk by the time we got back to the house. We put the grass into the bull's stable, then sat outside and ate sunflower seeds. As the villagers left the fields, another goat-related confrontation took place. One old woman accused another of letting her goats eat other people's crops. She shouted this accusation, because she was partially deaf, but it made the other woman shout back.

'It's just what goats do,' she yelled.

'No, it's not. I had goats and a water buffalo and they never ate anyone's vegetables.'

'Why are you angry? It's not your crops that have been eaten!'

The accuser had no answer for this, other than a drawn-out noise of contempt.

'They have this argument a lot,' said Weiping. 'It is like a hobby.'

We went inside and watched ping-pong, then snooker on the huge old TV. Just as we were about to go to bed, there was a loud banging on the door. Weiping's grandfather had come to tell him that his uncle had been put in jail for gambling.

'He'll get five days in jail and a fine,' he said, with what sounded like approval.

In the night I woke and needed the toilet. I took a torch and went out past his grandfather's house. Hearing me, he yelled, 'I can't sleep!'

'Me too,' I replied. On the way back to the house I stopped and turned off the torch. There was just the calling of frogs, the stars in their multitudes.

*

By lunchtime the following day Weiping had given out another thousand yuan. Almost half went to his father, but three other people – two cousins and an uncle – got several hundred each. At the time Weiping didn't complain, but later he seemed bothered. 'This is why some young people hate going home,' he said.

It was perhaps to avoid giving out any more money that he suggested going for a walk. We didn't get far before a car offered us a lift. Inside were a young couple returning to their jobs in Guangzhou. They were working in Baiyun ('White Cloud') district, a northern suburb I was due to visit, as Da Ming, my former student, was now living there. The car was packed with fruit and food they were taking back. 'It's much better than the food in Guangzhou,' they said. I asked if they planned to move there permanently. 'No,' said the woman. 'It's just a place to work. Our families are here.'

There's a widespread assumption that most migrants want to settle down in the cities, but in recent years an increasing number of surveys have suggested that many don't want to. One study found that only 40 per cent of migrant workers in Beijing had any interest in staying there permanently.[7] This also explains why many migrant workers in Beijing stay in poor-quality accommodation even when they could afford slightly better housing – it's just a temporary place to live. There are also indications that a large number of migrants want to remain rural citizens. A study by the Sichuan provincial statistics bureau found that 90 per cent of the migrants they interviewed wanted to keep their rural *hukou*.[8] In the absence of any national welfare system, having the entitlement to use the land that a rural *hukou* affords is viewed by many migrants as an essential safety net.

But this doesn't mean that China's dwindling villages are going to be repopulated by returning migrant workers. Many of the younger, second generation of migrants have little experience of farming, and so will have to find non-agricultural work, which may be scarce in small towns given the lack of investment in rural industry. This is arguably a direct result of the economic boom in manufacturing in the southern coastal provinces in the mid-1990s. Before then the most vibrant parts of the Chinese economy were Township and Village Enterprises (TVEs), small companies run by local governments.[9] In 1978, when the economic reform period began,

TVEs employed 28 million; by 1996, 135 million were working for them. But this was the apogee of TVEs – from the mid-1990s the state was more interested in promoting foreign-owned businesses on the east coast. Banks stopped lending to TVEs, which then couldn't compete with private businesses. Essentially, the Chinese state decided that most of its own enterprises weren't profitable enough to help the economy grow, never mind the fact that these were employing a large proportion of the working-age population. If the TVEs hadn't been so thoroughly marginalised, China's migrant population probably wouldn't be so large: there would have been jobs far closer to home.

There certainly weren't a lot of employment options near Weiping's village. We got out of the car at a crossroads by a small factory that looked half-demolished. Its windows were missing and some walls had been knocked down; the roof was sagging badly. But there was a yellow digger in the yard and several mounds of earth and gravel. A small cloud of smoke suggested work was going on.

'This used to be a weapons factory,' said Weiping. 'They made bullets, I think.' He turned and pointed to some brick buildings down the road. Cables dangled from the walls and roof and most of the windows were missing; some had been covered with plastic sheeting from the inside.

'When I was young, many soldiers lived in those buildings. Now the people in there work in a lead mine in the hills.'

Weiping's bossy neighbour's son worked in this mine at night. Zetao was a softly spoken man with a pensive air who, unlike many other people in the village, had gone to senior middle school. He hadn't wanted to be a miner, but this had been his father's job and when he died, Zetao had been forced to carry on in the position. Mining is one of the most dangerous jobs in China, and there are frequent fatalities. Ten years ago, the biggest employer in the area was a coal mine, but after a major accident it had closed. Zetao seemed resigned to his job. 'It's hard, but there's no choice,' he said.

However, the mine wasn't the only local employment option. Weiping and I found another in an old factory nearby that looked as if it was under siege. The building was surrounded by long rows of what appeared to be wooden stakes, propped up and facing in opposite directions like a cheval-de-frise. As we got closer we saw they were thinly cut sheets of wood coiled into tubes. We picked our way between the lines and walked into a warehouse. Thin sheets of wood were piled six feet high in a cavernous space that was deserted. If we'd been timber thieves, we'd have made a killing.

A mechanical saw started nearby. As we went towards it the sound quickly died; when we stepped into a large room off the back of the warehouse the blades were barely spinning. It was a gloomy room with a crumbling ceiling, the centre of which was dominated by two long wood-cutting tables. Aprons, hats and several chainsaws were hanging on hooks on the walls. Two men stood by the now-stopped saw. One held a long piece of uncut wood next to the blade, while the other stood slightly back and had a large bunch of keys on his belt. I asked if he was the owner, suddenly aware we'd walked into his factory uninvited.

'Yes,' he said frostily. 'It's mine.'

'Have you been here long?'

'Seven years.'

'And are you from here?'

'No, I'm from Shaoyang.'

'Me too!' I said, then quickly amended my falsehood. 'I used to work there as a teacher.'

'Oh,' he said and smiled, my Shaoyang tenure apparently vouching for me.

'So why did you come here to open a factory?'

'I heard there were a lot of good pine trees here.' His gaze drifted out of the window. I followed it and saw trees, piles of lumber, a man welding the back of a truck without eye protection.

'It's a good business. Maybe I will repair this building.'

He pointed to the roof, through which I saw patches of sky. We wandered outside and saw two middle-aged women with weathered faces pushing a laden cart between lines of drying wood. Together they picked up a tube of paper, carefully unrolled it, then pressed the wood flat. The cart was already stacked five feet high, and looked heavy to lift, but they laughed when I asked if it was hard work.

'Oh no,' said one of the women, who was wearing a fetching pink jacket over whose arms she had pulled bright blue sleeve protectors. 'It's much easier than planting rice. And we earn more – two thousand yuan a month.'

'She's right,' said the other woman, while smoothing out the wood.

We went back home and cut more grass for the bull, then put it in the stable. As the light faded, the animals and their humans started coming home. First, the woman with the unruly goats, then a lady leading a water buffalo. We saw the workers from the wood factory, who waved; then, when it was almost dark, the bull lumbered past.

Weiping's father came to say goodbye – I was leaving for Changsha the next day – followed by a pretty young woman with a baby who had been a school classmate of Weiping's. Like him, Shiwen had been away, but she'd been in Guangzhou. She'd been working in McDonald's while her mother-in-law looked after her baby. Though Shiwen didn't earn a high wage – about as much as the women in the wood factory – she'd liked being in Guangzhou.

'So why did you come back?' he asked.

'I had to because my mother-in-law died after being hit by a car. The driver was the local Communist Party secretary, who had commissioned my father-in-law to make a building, then refused to pay him when it was completed. After my in-laws demanded he pay, he threatened to have them killed. A month later he ran them down. He did go to prison for this, but now his son is the new Party secretary.'

She said this more in sorrow than anger. Neither she nor Weiping spoke for a moment. Then her baby wailed, and for the next few minutes she was trying to distract it from crying. When it was pacified, she said, 'It's hard to be a mother,' without any bitterness.

I asked if she had plans to go back to Guangzhou.

'There's no way,' she said, but smiled.

7

THE BUBBLE

Although most of my students wanted to go south to Guangdong province, there were a few who meant to stay in Hunan. Their goal was to find work or do further study in Changsha, the provincial capital. It was a more modest dream, and certainly less risky, not least because they'd be nearer their parents. It was also a less daunting prospect than going south to a huge city where they'd know few people. I used to think of Changsha as a grander version of Shaoyang. It may be the provincial capital of Hunan, with three times the population, but it too is a port city with more than two thousand years of history. Changsha spreads along the east bank of the Xiang River; like Shaoyang, it is in an especially fertile area. In both cities some of the most prestigious institutions were set up by foreigners. In Shaoyang, it was the first hospital; in Changsha, Yale graduates set up a school in 1906 that still ranks among the country's top 100. In both places these institutions stemmed from the efforts of Christian missionaries, though this wasn't unopposed: in 1891 Griffith John, an Englishman, was stoned by a mob when he tried to enter Changsha. It was an experience that led him to regard it as 'one of the few places left in the whole world which no foreigner may presume to enter'.[1]

In Changsha, as in Shaoyang, there were also quiet places where I could sit without becoming the centre of attention. I confess that one of these was McDonald's, where I spent hours drinking milkshakes and stared in wonder at any other foreigner who happened to come in (it was usually months since I'd seen one). A far better place was Orange Island, a long sandbank in the middle of the river. According to one Chinese tourism company, 'it absolutely looks like a green naval vessel, sailing in the center of Changsha and ready to defend the old town.'[2] Though there were small buildings there, I saw very few people. Like Mao Zedong – who often went there when he was studying in the city in the 1920s – I was able to stretch out by the water and sunbathe.

While Leiyang has some grounds for being thought a 'red' place, with a long Communist tradition, Changsha has a much greater claim. In addition to Mao, many other top leaders of the People's Republic of China, such as Hu Yaobang, Liu Shaoqi and Zhu Rongji have come from the Changsha area, as well as the Communist icon Lei Feng. All Chinese schoolchildren are taught Lei Feng's story as a praiseworthy example. He was a soldier who spent his life slaving at menial tasks because of his love for Chairman Mao (some scholars argue that the tale is entirely made up). A telephone pole crushed him to death in 1962. In 1963 a propaganda campaign exhorted people to 'Follow the examples of Comrade Lei Feng'. There is even a special Lei Feng day on 5 March when people are supposed to perform acts of community service, like cleaning parks or helping the elderly. The day after one of these occasions, I asked my students if they had done anything in the spirit of Lei Feng. Most laughed and said no, which angered the few students who were Communist Youth League members. 'No, this is very serious, very important!' one boy shouted, possibly because he thought it was expected of him. But when I asked the class if they wanted to have a life like Lei Feng's, not even the League members said yes.

The wider disillusionment with notions of suffering personal hardship for the common good was underlined by the failure of three films released in 2013 to commemorate the 50th anniversary of the Lei Feng campaign.[3] In some cities not a single ticket was sold on the first day. One cinema in Beijing sold 43 tickets for one of the films, but it took four days. Ten times that number of tickets was sold for the *Les Misérables* film (which I suppose you could argue is evidence that the Chinese public *are* interested in revolutionary narratives, so long as they feature Anne Hathaway). While the idea of the Chinese Dream as a national project may resonate with many Chinese people, their response to Lei Feng suggests a lack of interest in self-sacrifice as a means to achieve this goal.

But the parallels between Shaoyang and Changsha only go so far. Though the city has a long history, few buildings in the city are more than 80 years old. The main reason for this is that, in 1938, the city was deliberately burned. The Nationalist authorities thought Changsha was going to be conquered by the Japanese, and decided to destroy the city's supplies. Unfortunately, they miscalculated; the city didn't fall to the Japanese until 1944. A British doctor recalled seeing soldiers breaking down the doors of houses while holding oil-soaked rags, setting them on fire, then opening the windows of the houses to spread the flames quicker.[4] In the ensuing blaze, which burned for three days, over 20,000 people died and about two-thirds of the city's buildings were destroyed. In the words of an American missionary present at that time, Changsha 'lay flat, wrecked, and totally vulnerable'.[5]

When I visited the city in 1999 there were few clues to its apocalyptic history – the first memorial to the fire wasn't erected until 2005. What remained of the city's past was being swiftly erased by construction. Between 2000 and 2010 the population of the city almost doubled. When I returned to the city in late 2014, I initially found nothing I recognised save the river. Even in Beijing, despite the violent paroxysms of demolition leading up to the Olympics, there had still been recognisable aspects of the city left (not least because no one will ever be allowed to build apartments on Tiananmen Square). In Changsha even the road layout seemed different, as if an entire new city had been grafted on top of the old.

Of course, this wasn't true – after a few hours walking around I realised that behind the grand hotels and towers lining the major streets there were still old apartment complexes. Changsha also has a protected old area with small houses where cats slink over the roofs, and narrow alleys that make 90-degree turns. In the one-room Buddhist temples the air is hazy with smoke from hanging spirals of incense. Another reason the zone is protected is that from 1937 to 1938 it was the headquarters of the Korean government-in-exile, which was originally based in Shanghai but had to move due to persecution from the Japanese army.

Unfortunately, this area seems to be the high point of Changsha's attempts at historical preservation. Perhaps the most egregious disregard for the city's history was the recent demolition of a thousand-year-old section of Changsha's city walls during the construction of a luxury apartment building by the Wanda Group, one of China's largest commercial property developers. Afterwards, one Weibo user commented: 'After a few more years we would have nothing left. 5000 years of Chinese history, what a joke, 5000 years and all people see are steel and concrete buildings?'[6]

The city government certainly intends to keep development heading in that direction; in July 2012 they unveiled plans for a 130-billion-dollar set of projects including airport expansion, road building and waste treatment.[7] Even allowing for a degree of exaggeration (officials tend to get promoted according to the economic performance of their region), this would still be a major economic stimulus for the city. Before this Changsha had a good economy – in 2011, its economy grew by 15 per cent, nearly twice the national rate. A large part of this is attributed to its thriving cultural sector. The local TV station, usually known as Hunan TV, has been responsible for launching a number of incredibly popular *American Idol*-like audition shows, especially *Chao Ji Nu Sheng*

(*Super Girl*) and *Kuai Le Nan Sheng* (*Super Boy*). In 2014 Hunan
TV was the highest-rated provincial TV network in China; only
CCTV, the national network, had more viewers.

Changsha may be far behind cities like Beijing or Shanghai,
but with its malls and Starbucks and nine-screen cinemas it feels
vastly removed from places like Shaoyang or Leiyang. It even has
a metro – the first line opened on the day I arrived. At the ticket
machines, young people wearing red waistcoats with Lei Feng's face
on them were helping passengers. On the walls, colourful adverts
warned against corruption. One showed giant calipers for measur-
ing prison sentences; another had a spiral of offences that ended
in a pair of handcuffs.

As a provincial capital, Changsha's *hukou* requirements are
likely to exclude a lot of people, but its reasonable property prices
have made it attractive to those who can't afford to live in the big
east-coast cities. Changsha can be thought of as a success story,
but its growth has left it with problems common to many Chinese
cities. Its public transport system is overcrowded, the roads are
often gridlocked and, like almost three-quarters of Chinese cities,
the air is dangerously polluted. This isn't helped by a lack of public
green spaces and few dedicated lanes for cyclists. It's also struggling
to cope with providing healthcare for so many new city residents. I
went to Hunan Cancer Hospital, one of the city's top hospitals, to
find out how they were likely to cope with potentially having tens
of thousands of new patients.

The hospital was built in 1972 and is the main centre for oncol-
ogy in the province. When I arrived, people were selling medicine
on the pavement outside. One seller claimed to have been cured of
brain cancer; another was offering pills he said could cure diabetes.
In the hospital courtyard the medical market continued – a man
had two live turtles on a string and was trying to sell them to people
going into the building. He was interrupted by a hospital security
guard, who seemed about to make the man leave, but then engaged

him in conversation. After a few minutes, the guard bought one of the turtles.

Low-level chaos reigned within the entrance hall. Patients in gowns with shaved heads wandered round or hovered near a woman pushing a food trolley. Visitors, patients and medical staff crowded around the lifts. Children in wheelchairs and people on crutches kept cutting through the queue for the hospital dispensary. In a corner an old man smoked furtively next to a machine for patient feedback. I'd been in many hospitals in China before, but had never seen one as busy as this. Over lunch Dr Li, who'd been working in the hospital for a decade, told me that in recent years the hospital had been struggling to cope with a rise in patient numbers.

'In 2003 they made cheap health insurance available to anyone, and most people are taking advantage of it. We are getting more and more busy. It's very hard to manage so many patients.'

Dr Li adjusted the collar of her white blouse; on it there were small green stones that caught the light. She wore rimless glasses and her eyes looked tired. She was married, had a nine-year-old daughter, and was a native of Changsha. I asked where most of her patients came from.

'The majority, maybe 70 per cent, come from the countryside. The insurance doesn't cover people from outside the province. It also doesn't cover everything. For some diseases they will pay 80 per cent of the cost. The insurance often doesn't pay for outpatient care either.'

Two weeks of chemotherapy can cost 100,000 yuan (around $15,000) in Hunan Cancer Hospital, so the shortfall is a huge problem for many patients. But the poor standard of healthcare in the countryside means that urban hospitals will still be the first choice for many patients, even if it means amassing huge debts.

I asked Dr Li if the hospital would be able to cope with more and more patients.

'Yes,' she said, and sounded confident. 'But all of us doctors are overworked and there is too much paperwork. I also think the cancer rate has increased. This is partly due to increased awareness and better screening of patients. But people's changing diet and the environmental pollution are also playing a role.'

Urban hospitals aren't just having to cope with more patients – there's also been a rise in the prevalence of obesity and related diseases like diabetes. People in Chinese cities tend to eat more food, and usually of a lower quality: Kentucky Fried Chicken is the country's number one food chain. The increased consumption of junk food, and the adoption of a more sedentary lifestyle, has meant that within one generation the amount of overweight or obese children in China has risen from 5 to 20 per cent,[8] a shocking increase – though still not as bad as in the US, where a third of all children and adolescents are overweight or obese.[9]

Funding is a major problem for public hospitals in China. Most rely on drug sales for their revenue, which has led to overcharging patients for medicine and prescribing unnecessary drugs.[10] Doctors' low pay also makes them susceptible to bribes from drug companies, as well as from patients and relatives seeking preferential treatment. The Chinese government has pledged to eliminate the markup on drugs, but so far it's only focusing on smaller, county-level hospitals. A few of these, in desperation, have attempted to get drug companies to pay a large 'deposit', sometimes as much as tens of thousands of dollars per product. In October 2015 Jiangsu Province Hospital requested that companies pay 8 per cent of their annual in-hospital sales in advance, and although some Chinese drug companies complied, few international ones agreed. As a result, some drugs were unavailable at the hospital, which provoked patient complaints and attracted media attention. In January 2016 the hospital reversed the ban on these drugs.[11]

Public confidence in China's healthcare system remains low – it's telling that, of the five pledges to patients listed on the Hunan

Cancer Hospital's website, four address issues of corruption, over-charging and using 'fake and inferior' medicines.[12]

The rising cost of medical fees has resulted in a corresponding rise in patient expectations, and in violent confrontations with hospital staff.[13] In 2010 there were 17,000 such incidents (a 70 per cent increase from 2005). In 2011, a calligrapher stabbed a doctor 17 times because he was unhappy with his treatment. In March 2012 a patient in Harbin who had been refused a drug killed a doctor with a hammer and knife. When the *People's Daily* newspaper posted an online poll asking people to express their reaction to the murder by picking a happy face, a sad one or one with an angry expression, most chose the face that was smiling.[14]

According to Doctor Li, this kind of public anger was another reason for the shortage of doctors: 'Parents are telling their children not to be doctors because they think it is dangerous. There have already been many terrible incidents this year.'

Less than two months before, in three separate incidents within a fortnight, a nurse had been attacked and paralysed, a doctor's throat had been slashed, and another doctor beaten to death with a lead pipe. Doctor Li wasn't optimistic about doctor–patient relations improving.

'Patients have wrong expectations, and doctors don't have time to explain, so it will go on.'

I asked her why she had wanted to be a doctor.

'I don't know. My uncle was a doctor. My parents thought it would be a good job for me.' She smiled ruefully. 'And so I was jailed in this hospital.'

Would she encourage her daughter to be a doctor in Changsha?

'If she wants to, it is OK. But I won't suggest it.'

*

To understand how Changsha has managed to grow so fast – and why this is risky – you need only climb to the top floor of any of the tall buildings near the city's second ring road. From the 33rd floor, looking vertiginously down, I saw huge holes in the ground where construction workers were labouring in the shade of colourful beach umbrellas. Raising my gaze, I saw a nearby trio of concrete towers pushing upwards like the pins of a plug. In the near distance, on the far bank of the river, at least 100 finished apartment buildings, all 30 storeys tall, were laid out in formation. Whichever direction I looked in, there was more of the same.

In 2015 China built 58 per cent of the global total of skyscrapers, according to a report by the Council on Tall Buildings and Urban Habitat.[15] In theory this construction frenzy makes sense: the millions of new urban residents that are envisaged will need to live somewhere. And from the perspective of most city authorities, this continued construction is essential for their finances. The revenue from land sales pays for, on average, 60 per cent of the municipal budget (and in some cities, like Changsha, almost 100 per cent). The upshot is that funding for most services provided by city authorities is inextricably tied to the performance of their property markets.

One might argue that in a country with a predicted 250 million new urban residents this isn't an awful risk; surely there will be no shortage of demand for housing. But in reality, there's a lack of affordable housing for the majority (a problem facing cities as disparate as London and San Francisco). Between 2000 and 2010 the national average house price in China increased by 250 per cent.[16] Though the government has said it wants a fifth of all housing to be reserved for low-income residents, this is once again something migrants will be excluded from: affordable housing is usually reserved for people with a local *hukou*[17] (admittedly not a problem facing Londoners).

In cities like Beijing and Shanghai only the wealthy have any chance of buying property. Elsewhere, though the prices aren't as exorbitant, the housing market is still aimed at the affluent, many of whom buy property as an investment. But even with a second home ownership rate higher than many European countries (in 2007 in China it was already 15 per cent, more than in France, Germany or Holland), there's still a massive housing surplus.[18]

This has been most starkly evident in the phenomenon of 'ghost cities', new urban developments with very low occupancy rates. These have inspired a glut of photo galleries of deserted streets and squares, and a series of gloomy (and sometimes gleeful) pronouncements about the End of the Chinese Economic Miracle. Some of these new cities will probably fail, but it's likely that many will end up being viable urban centres. One reason it's so common to see vacant apartment buildings in China is that about 80 per cent of new apartments are sold before construction is finished, and most are sold unfurnished as well.[19] Defenders of these new urban projects (which in many cases are like new twin cities for existing ones) also argue that these big projects will *create* the necessary demand, though in some cases this seems wildly optimistic: Tianjin is projected to have more office space than can be utilised in the next 25 years, at least at the current rate.[20]

In the Doubleday Compound in Changsha about half of the apartments were empty three years after construction had finished. When I went outside and sat on a bench there was no one around; the only sound was the flickering of paper fans attached to the palm trees. Five minutes later a woman in her sixties pushing a pram sat down on the next bench. When I asked if she lived in the compound, she pointed to a fifth-floor flat.

'I've been there two years,' she said. 'It's good, but sometimes there's a lot of noise from the Beijing–Guangzhou train.'

Weiying was a retired government official. Every afternoon she pushed her granddaughter around the plaza. She'd been able to afford the expensive apartment because government workers could buy at a subsidised price.

'I had to buy out here because I needed more space. But my friends are all in town. It's too quiet here. At least half of these apartments are empty because people have only bought them as an investment.'

She admitted she was sometimes lonely living in an apartment complex with so few neighbours. 'But it would be worse without my granddaughter or my dog. When people see her they come and talk to me. If I didn't have a dog or a child, I wouldn't know anyone.'

Later that evening I had dinner with Fan Di, an estate agent in one of the city's biggest property firms. She admitted that in Changsha there was a surplus of housing, but didn't think it was a problem.

'We aim for 70 per cent occupancy in the first year, but only need a 50 per cent occupancy rate to break even. What people want is to live away from the centre but have good links to it. The subway is crucial, and so is school access.'

She'd just bought an apartment herself, at a huge new development outside town called Meixi Lake. We went there the next day and walked around the edge of the large, artificial lake. The water had an odd, bright blue-green hue reminiscent of swimming pools. On the opposite bank a line of pink villas were dwarfed by the identical towers behind them, which at the far left were finished but as one looked right seemed to be degenerating into progressively less complete versions of themselves, until there was just a shaft of concrete wrapped in green netting with a crane as chaperone. In the distance the cranes continued on the near and far shore until they were lost in the distant haze.

When finished, Meixi Lake is projected to provide homes (or second homes) for 180,000 people and be the residential centre of a new business district.[21] The centrepiece of the development will be an international culture and arts centre designed by Zaha Hadid. The plans for the centre show three petal-like buildings that seem so futuristic they belong on Mars. While its lake looks fake, and the landscaping was rushed – the small ripples of the water were already eroding the shore – overall the surrounding park is still a peaceful place for anyone to enjoy. I saw a lot of people walking or sitting in its grounds who didn't look like they could afford to buy a property there.

Changsha's building frenzy was due to culminate in Sky City, a 220-floor tower that would have been China's tallest building. The project broke ground in 2013, but was then halted due to problems with building permits and safety concerns. Two years later construction remained suspended; local people were using the foundation pits as a fish farm. In June 2016 it was announced that the project had been dropped due to concerns about the environmental impact on the surrounding wetlands, which have since been designated a no-construction zone.

Behind all the grand rhetoric of the Chinese Dream, the future for China's cities (and their actual and potential residents) arguably comes down to whether or not the property market can be kept healthy. This means that the market mustn't become so inflated that the property bubble pops, nor become so deflated that land sales don't generate enough revenue for the cities. Too many empty houses will discourage developers from starting new projects, which would mean a loss of wages for workers, lower orders to suppliers of construction materials, and thus less business for suppliers of anything one buys for a house. If this happens, it's likely to lead to China's economy crashing again, the consequences of which will affect everyone. As the world's second largest economy, and the second largest importer of both goods and commercial services, virtually every other economy will feel the pinch as well.

So how healthy is China's property market? It has certainly slowed down considerably since late 2011, though it's hard to speak of national trends when property prices in places like Beijing, Changsha and Shaoyang differ so much. In the most affluent cities the markets recovered considerably in 2015, but those in smaller and medium-sized cities are still struggling.[22] This partial recovery was helped by the central government cutting interest rates and offering tax reductions to buyers. The success of this measure illustrates how good the Chinese government is at heating up and cooling down the property market to suit its needs, which is one reason why the so-called property bubble in China isn't likely to pop. Another is that some further loosening of the *hukou* system, at least in terms of home ownership, seems likely to occur in the next three to five years. In 2015 Premier Li Keqiang told a cabinet meeting that changes are needed to allow more people with rural *hukou* into the cities in order to boost the housing market.

A trial version of this idea is currently under way in several cities. In the cities of Longyan in Fujian province and Tongling in Anhui province, some rural residents have been allowed to buy property without having to give up their rural *hukou* and the land entitlements that go with it. In the next few years Chinese cities will either loosen or tighten their *hukou* requirements depending on the state of their property markets. In some cases this may finally allow migrants to get to buy homes in the cities they helped build.

8

THE VILLAGE IN THE CITY

It was hard to hear Peimeng above the noise of mah-jong. We were in a large sun-filled room in which elderly people sat hunched over felt-covered tables. When a game ended, the tiles were furiously mixed together with a rumbling collision that obscured his voice. He was telling me about his childhood in a fishing village on China's south coast in the 1970s. Although the neon lights of Hong Kong were only 20 kilometres away, at night the small houses in his village were completely engulfed by the dark. If the villagers needed to buy salt or sugar, they had to walk ten kilometres to a small market town. They didn't go more than two or three times a year; when they did they bought fabric to make new clothes.

When Peimeng was 15 he started working for the village production unit. 'My main jobs were separating wheat, planting yams and extracting peanut oil,' he recalled 40 years later. He did not remember the work as being especially hard. 'It was no problem. It's Chinese culture,' he said and nodded in approval. Peimeng had a plump, satisfied face and was wearing an expensive-looking purple-and-blue-striped shirt with the top button done up. We were talking in the recreation centre for elderly people in his village, although it was a village in name only. Outside there were no paddy fields, just the skyscrapers of Shenzhen, China's fifth-biggest city.

No city better encapsulates China's economic miracle since the late 1970s than Shenzhen. Before 1980 there were only 300,000 people in the area; in 2014 around 11 million people lived in the city. Shenzhen was where China broke decisively with Maoist ideology and embraced capitalism in order to develop an export economy. Over the next three decades the combination of cheap migrant labour, easy access to raw materials, and investment from Hong Kong would make the city synonymous with China's economic transformation. Even the financial crash of 2008 didn't dent its prosperity – Shenzhen had already started shifting its economy from manufacturing into finance and high-end technology. Wang Yang, the leader of Guangdong province, said it was necessary to 'empty the bird cage for new birds to settle down'.[1] The new birds he had in mind were companies like the telecoms giant Huawei and Tencent, China's largest internet service portal, who are now both based in Shenzhen. In 2014 the GDP per capita of its Nanshan district was higher than Germany, Japan and Hong Kong; the city's overall economy was worth 1.6 trillion yuan.[2]

Migrants from the countryside often lack the skills and education to find non-agricultural work in cities. But in the early 1980s anyone living in one of Shenzhen's 320 villages was already in possession of the most valuable resource: land. They didn't own it individually, but as rural land it was under the control of their village collective. If the land had been classified as urban, the municipal authorities would have been able to evict them; instead, the villagers had control over prime development sites in the centre of modern China's biggest economic experiment.

In some villages people leased land to factories from Hong Kong, or set up their own businesses.[3] One village in Futian dug up sand from nearby land and sold it to construction sites; another imported used tyres from Hong Kong for recycling. But Peimeng's village was cautious at first, remembering that during the Maoist era many people suffered when official policy was reversed and they found themselves accused of being either 'reactionary' or 'ultra-left'. Peimeng said there were few changes to the village in the 1980s, except for a few people who added an extra floor to their houses for their own use.

'But in the 1990s we became brave,' he said. 'The land was ours, so we just started building.'

Though the maximum height for residential dwellings was three storeys, many villagers in Shenzhen added fourth and fifth floors to their houses. They rented these cheaply to migrant workers, most of whom lacked residence permits, and so benefited from the city's limited jurisdiction within the villages. Throughout the 1990s villagers in Shenzhen ignored the city's building codes, adding extra floors to their houses to maximise their rental income. People joked that the villagers no longer cared about planting crops for harvest – all they cared about was 'growing buildings'.

Few concessions were made to the need for such unprofitable things as wide streets or public spaces. When you walk through these neighbourhoods today the alleys are narrow and gloomy. The apartments are so close together that people call them 'kissing buildings'. To glimpse the sky you must crane your neck back and look up through washing and dripping air-conditioning units: only then will you see a thread of light.

These chaotic, often unsanitary developments (which became known as 'urban villages') didn't fit with the municipal authorities' image of Shenzhen as a shining, modern city, but they did solve the problem of how to house the hundreds of thousands of migrant workers needed for construction and factory work. At the start of the mass migration many workers lived in factory dormitories, but those without stable employment, who were self-employed, or who had brought their families, needed to rent their own apartments. Although the rents were cheap, the villagers still received a huge income. Peimeng had no doubts about the benefits of the changes.

'We used to be so poor that we had to borrow our salary in advance from the production group for Chinese New Year. Our annual household income before the reforms was around 900 yuan.

But after 1995, the opportunities to make money were everywhere. So it has been a golden age ever since.'

In the late 1990s the city authorities threatened to enforce the building regulations, but this only spurred people to add more floors to their houses, in the belief it would allow them to gain more compensation if their homes were demolished. By the 2000s many buildings in urban villages were ten storeys high. As a result, Shenzhen has the highest proportion of small-property accommodation in China, accounting for half of its total built-up area (in Beijing it's only 20 per cent, and in Xi'an 30 per cent).

Eventually the government offered to recognise village buildings as legal if households paid a small penalty and agreed to the land being redesignated as urban. This meant the villagers could no longer pass on the land via inheritance, but still allowed them 'land-use rights' (which expire after 70 years). This concept actually originated in Shenzhen – before 1988 the Chinese constitution prohibited selling or renting land. But in 1987 the Shenzhen government held the first public auction of land-use rights, and made sure that everyone noticed by inviting Communist Party officials, the mayors of 17 other cities, and the media. The following year, the Chinese constitution was amended, allowing land to become a commodity. This was arguably the start of China's great urban transformation – it made buying, selling and developing land into hugely profitable enterprises.

After Peimeng's village became urban land, there was technically no village. In most other parts of China this would probably have led to the fragmentation of community, mainly because urban residents don't usually control their own land-use rights so can be evicted. But what happened in Shenzhen was an inversion of the great rural migration to the cities – it was the city that came to them. This allowed the village to preserve much of its identity. Spatially, the villagers remained close to each other, albeit vastly outnumbered by migrants. Peimeng said there were around 200,000 people living in his urban village, only a thousand of whom weren't migrants. But although they only made up 0.5 per cent of the area's population, the villagers were still a cohesive unit. Many urban villages are essentially clan-based societies, where the majority of the residents are from a small number of families whose shared ancestry goes back hundreds of years. Peimeng's ancestors had been in the area for 600 years – he was the 26th generation of the Jiang family.

Later that day he took me to the temple devoted to his ancestors. Such temples are common throughout south China, and serve as a visible reminder of a family's lineage. Inside there were prayers on the walls asking for a good harvest, great prosperity and protection from harm. Next to these was a long list of names of people who had contributed money to the temple. When I asked him whether it brought him luck to live so close to the temple of his ancestors, he said, 'For me, I think so. But some people who aren't from the village don't like it. Some of them worry about ghosts.'

In addition to sentiment and familial loyalty, the residents of most urban villages are tied by financial bonds. Many villages formed shareholding companies that are responsible for managing their properties and which often work with property developers. They also frequently own a number of subsidiary enterprises. The most prosperous of these shareholding companies was started by a villager called Pan Qiang'en, from Wanfeng village.[4] By 2008 the Wanfeng Stock Company was worth over $130 million and had 60,000 employees working in electronics, plastics, clothing, paper and toy production. Though Peimeng's village company wasn't as successful, the villagers still received a huge income.

'The average monthly income per household is between 200,000 and 500,000 yuan per month. The lowest income is just over 10,000 yuan per month, but the owner of that property has a gambling addiction.'

These huge profits have allowed many urban villages to function like *danwei*. Though the villagers are now legally urban residents, it's the village company, not the Shenzhen authorities, that takes care of their welfare. Many provide heavily subsidised healthcare and social security benefits. Peimeng's village also provided private security and schooling for the villagers, and had paid for the construction of the elderly persons' social centre. Anyone walking by could look through its large windows and see the oldest villagers drinking tea and eating fruit while squabbling over mah-jong or card games. They could see the large ornately framed pieces of calligraphy on the walls (some of them done by Peimeng). To many passers-by, it must have looked like an exclusive club.

I asked Peimeng if anyone resented the villagers earning so much without having to work. He thought for a moment, then said, 'Back when people had less, things were quite peaceful. Nowadays, with greater wealth, people compare with each other. People have started to lose their mental balance.'

According to Peimeng, there were few problems between migrants and the villagers, because Shenzhen was a tolerant and open place. I didn't catch what he said next because an elderly woman came and stood in front of me. Her skin was thinly stretched over her cheeks and she spoke quickly in Cantonese. When I didn't respond, she lapsed into silence, then wandered to the end of the room.

'What did she say?' I asked Peimeng.

'She doesn't recognise you and wants to know what you are doing in the village.'

She came back and said something else, then made a scooping motion with her hand in front of my face. She seemed agitated. Peimeng said, 'This woman isn't from my village. She has dementia and comes here sometimes. I don't understand most of what she's saying now.'

We sat, somewhat awkwardly, while she scooped the air. When she walked away, I asked Peimeng if he was worried about the city trying to revoke their usage rights, or just confiscating the land without paying sufficient compensation. In 2005 the city announced an urban village redevelopment programme whose ultimate goal was a 'city without urban villages'. Both the Shenzhen media and the city authorities have since demonised urban villages. The *Shenzhen Special Economic Zone News* described urban villages as 'dirty, chaotic and inferior' and called them an 'urban malignant tumour'.[5] This hyperbole was prompted by the local government's fear that there won't be enough land available for big investors – cheap (or even free) land is the best incentive it has to get major companies to stay in or relocate to Shenzhen. The local government was so determined to prevent Huawei leaving Shenzhen that in 2010 it gifted the company a 22-square-kilometre area to use as its new headquarters.[6]

But Peimeng wasn't worried. 'Even if the government wants to rebuild the village, they must purchase the land at market value. The land belongs to the village shareholder company and so we must be compensated with money and equivalent-value housing.'

When I brought up the fact that in other cities the compensation paid has generally been far below market value, Peimeng responded that because the village shareholding companies hold the use rights, they must be properly compensated. This fact seems to have protected many urban villages in Shenzhen from the attentions of property development companies. The costs and uncertainties of redeveloping an urban village are considerably greater than for a plot of land owned by the city, which has made property developers hesitant to get involved in such projects. For the foreseeable future, urban villages are likely to remain a vital part of Shenzhen.

*

Shenzhen was created as the exception to the economic rule, and as such is perhaps the perfect example of Deng Xiaoping's pragmatic approach to governance, epitomised by his maxim, 'It doesn't matter if a cat is black or white, so long as it catches mice.' Shenzhen is also unlike other large Chinese cities because it's generally a pleasant place to live (not least because of its good air quality). Its residents are less vulnerable to the attempts of property developers and the local government to demolish and rebuild large swathes of the city whatever the social or environmental cost.

But perhaps Shenzhen's greatest boast is that there's less discrimination against migrants than in other major cities. Shanshan, a 45-year-old woman who worked as a cleaner, told me that Shenzhen had by far the most relaxed attitude to outsiders she had encountered. She was originally from the countryside near Chengdu, in Sichuan province, and had left home when she was 17. She'd gone to work as a waitress in Shanxi province, and hadn't stayed long.

'I wasn't used to noodles,' she said and laughed. She was happy because she was going to fly to Macao for a holiday later that day, and looked to have bought a new outfit. She was dressed entirely in white; on the shoulders of her jacket there were shining silver buckles. Her white shoes had sky-blue bows that made them look like presents.

From Shanxi she went to Jiangsu province, which she had liked much better. 'I thought about staying there and getting married.'

'Had you met someone?'

'No, but it was a good place. The only reason I left was because my mother got sick and I had to go back to Sichuan to take care of her. I have three sisters, but they were all married and living somewhere else. But it wasn't bad luck. If I hadn't gone back, I wouldn't have met my husband.'

Their first child was a girl, so they could have had another (the one-child policy allowed this only for female children). But Shanshan and her husband chose not to. 'I had three sisters, and growing up we didn't have enough food. It's better my daughter has what she needs.'

In 2001, when her daughter was still young, Shanshan and her husband moved to Shenzhen. Her first job was in a factory, but after three years she became a domestic cleaner. Her husband started as a construction worker, but soon worked his way up to become foreman, and later started handling construction project bids. He'd had to learn on the job, which Shanshan said had been very hard. She was proud of him.

Their daughter had mostly grown up in Shenzhen; for her it was home. When she and her parents went back to Sichuan to visit their relatives, she was unable to name any of the plants in the country-side. According to Shanshan, her daughter wouldn't need to go back to Sichuan to take the *gaokao* exam; Shenzhen lets children without a local *hukou* take the test with a 30-point handicap.

I asked Shanshan if she planned to ever go back to Sichuan.

'One day I will,' she said, but didn't sound certain. 'For now, life is very good here. Doesn't everyone want a better life?'

*

Kexin was also in no hurry to return to her home town. She'd come to Shenzhen from Shaoyang in 1993 and had remained there ever since. She was a teacher in an elementary school in Futian district. She'd started off as a primary teacher in Shaoyang but hadn't stayed long. Like Shanshan, she'd seen an opportunity and taken it.

'I wanted to improve my life, so I came here because it was more open.' Like Mr Ma, she'd needed permission to transfer, and although it hadn't been easy, it had only taken a year to arrange. When I told her about Mr Ma's seven-year wait, she laughed. 'It got more difficult later on. When I tried, there were more vacancies here, so it was easier to persuade people I should go.'

'Do you miss anything about Shaoyang?'

'My brother and sister and my friends. But I visit twice a year.'

I asked Kexin if she planned to go back when she retired.

'No, I'm used to it here. And I have good health insurance. The healthcare in Shenzhen is more advanced than in Hunan.'

Kexin had been teaching for 33 years, almost the entirety of China's post-reform period. I asked her what changes she'd seen in schools over that period.

'Kids back then were easy to tame and discipline, but they knew less. Now they have a strong sense of themselves, they are more confident, so harder to control. But they know more. Now we can focus on their whole development, their human quality. Not all schools focus on it, but that is the general trend.'

The idea of 'human quality' (in Chinese, *suzhi*) has been frequently invoked in China over the last few decades and is generally used to speak about personal development, how 'cultivated' a person is. While the term is used in different ways, it's generally employed in a hierarchical sense, i.e. some people are 'low quality' and others 'high quality'. The two types of people most commonly labelled 'low quality' are migrant workers and ethnic minorities. Apart from the Han, China's majority ethnic group, there are 55 other official recognised ethnic groups in China, who make up around eight per cent of the population. Many ethnic minorities' languages, cultures and traditions have been labelled 'backward' compared to that of the Han. With migrant workers, there's a similar kind of condescension.[7] The Chinese Dream, in terms of urbanisation, can thus be said to have a 'civilising' element to it – the idea being that making country people into urban citizens will raise their 'quality'.

By this logic, one might expect public schools to welcome migrants' children, so as to hasten their 'improvement'. But in Shenzhen, just as in Beijing, children without local *hukou* struggle to find state school places; only about 40 per cent attend state schools.[8] One reason is there aren't enough places – the number of schools depends on the number of people holding local *hukou*, and since the majority of people in Shenzhen don't have one, there's inevitably a huge shortfall. Another barrier is the bureaucratic requirements held by schools. Kexin said that migrant parents have to provide a lot of documents, such as residential leases, birth certificates and proof they have followed family-planning laws. Many parents don't have these and can't afford to obtain them. Even in a city where migrants are the majority, their children are thus forced to attend expensive, lower-quality private schools.

The lucky ones who do manage to get a place in a state school usually don't suffer the same degree of social exclusion as migrant children in other large cities. 'Shenzhen has no concept of outsiders because everyone is from somewhere else,' said the vice president of the Shenzhen Yuanhengjia Education Group, which runs more than a dozen pre-schools in the city.[9] Kexin also thought the children's ages were a factor. 'They are very young and so there's no prejudice,' she said. 'There are no differences between them.'

We looked out of the window of the school office down into a courtyard full of plants. Children in blue-and-white tracksuits were moving around quickly, almost running, because the school day was over. There was a knock on the door and a girl came in to speak to Kexin about the homework assignment. A moment later three other heads peeped round the door to look at me. I said hello and told the boy and two girls about myself, then asked if they were from Shenzhen. All three shook their heads.

'So where are you from?'

'Gansu.'

'Hunan.'

'Fujian.'

All three had started school in their home provinces before coming to join their parents in Shenzhen. The boy said that school in Hunan had been more relaxing, with less homework, but he still liked Shenzhen better because he was with his parents, although his father worked a lot.

'What does he do?'

'I don't know. He has never told me,' said the boy, and the two girls laughed. 'But I think it is something to do with buildings.'

We talked about which subjects they liked – all of them hated maths – then, at Kexin's urging, they took it in turns to ask me questions.

One of the girls asked, 'What's Halloween like? Is it terrifying?'

The other girl asked how often British students went camping.

The boy said, 'I have some dangerous pets, a snake and a spider. In the UK are there any dangerous animals?'

When I told him there weren't any, he looked disappointed. He rummaged in his rucksack and found a book with many colourful pictures of poisonous insects.

'What about this?' He pointed at a tarantula. 'Do you have it?' he said hopefully.

*

While there's less discrimination against migrants in Shenzhen, that doesn't mean the city has been entirely welcoming. When the Shenzhen Economic Zone (SEZ) was established, the authorities were so concerned about a flood of migrants that a barbed-wire fence was placed around the zone's four districts (Luohu, Futian, Yantian and Nanshan) to separate them from the adjoining Bao'an and Longgang districts. During the 2000s the border controls around the SEZ weakened, and in 2010 the barrier was abolished. The memory of the border persists in everyday speech – people in Shenzhen refer to the original four districts as *guan nei*, meaning 'within the border', and the outer districts as *guan wai* ('outside the border').

Though Shenzhen has allowed some people to switch their *hukou* to the city, it's been very selective about who can apply. In the mid-1990s it was possible for people who bought property in *guan wai* to shift their *hukou* there, and in 2012 Shenzhen admitted several hundred thousand college graduates as permanent residents.[10] Although allowing so many people to become permanent residents was unprecedented, and thus deserving of praise, there was no suggestion that construction workers, shop assistants or anyone else of low *suzhi* would be equally welcome.

The recent extension of the subway system into *guan wai* is eroding the gap between Shenzhen's inner and outer districts, but when I took the train north to Longhua New District (formerly a subdistrict of Bao'an), there was still an abrupt shift on leaving *guan nei*. The rows of apartments being built were interrupted by oases of undeveloped land. The new, wide roads around the Longhua underground station had the eerie blankness that accompanies large quantities of fresh concrete, but this was offset by the run-down three-storey buildings flanking them. Behind them was the sensory shock of an open-air market. It was a hot day and the smells were competing: chickens, fermented tofu, blood from pigs and cows. Vegetable sellers squirted water on cabbages; fish swam in polystyrene troughs until they were gutted. There were towers of red buckets and bowls, thickets of mops and brooms, a row of somersaulting toy dogs lined up on a sheet. A crowd moved between the stalls at a sluggish pace, parting only at the insistence of a scooter's horn. But the loudest sound was the amplified voice of a pickled turnip seller. He was using a small headset microphone to praise the quality of the turnips, the excellence of the price, the remarkable health benefits of eating turnips every day. He saw me watching him and added, 'Foreigners like them too!'

The market had a vibrancy and chaos absent from anywhere in *guan nei*, even the supposedly anarchic urban villages. But there were harbingers of the shape of things to come. Several people were handing out colourful flyers for new housing developments in the area. The price per square metre was printed in a huge font over a Photoshopped fantasy of what the finished apartments would look like. I'd been handed so many of these in different cities over the past few months – usually as I came off an escalator – that I'd acquired a vague sense of the average price, enough to know that the 4,000-yuan figure on one of them was incredibly cheap. The middle-aged woman giving them out saw my interest and started telling me that there were only four apartments left at that price. She was wearing a belted white jacket and floppy straw sun hat, and her voice was hoarse.

'Where is this?' asked a man who took a flyer.

'In Longgang district,' she replied.

'That's very far away.'

'No problem. I can get a car to take you; it will be less than two hours.'

'But where in Longgang is it?'

'In Daya Bay.'

The man handed the flier back. Daya Bay is home to six nuclear power stations, whose construction was fiercely opposed by local residents. In the wake of the Fukushima disaster in 2011 the Chinese public has been distrustful of nuclear power, which explained not only the low price of the property but also why the woman had travelled so far to try to find customers.

There were more successful selling techniques in the market. A trio of grey-robed Buddhist nuns were working the edge of the crowd. One approached me and opened a folder that contained a menu of prayer. I pointed at a picture of a red heart surrounded by dollar signs and said, 'That one.'

'Very good,' she replied. 'That will be 20 yuan.'

In my naivety, I hadn't realised she was *selling* the prayers. When I gave her the money she nodded and handed me a booklet featuring pictures of monks and their powerful auras, bright distortions of light around their heads that only a diehard sceptic could have mistaken for lens flare. But when I came back to the market later that day, I was glad I'd paid. The nun was holding tightly onto the arm of a thin young man wearing glasses who had refused to give her money. He was calling for help, and close to panic, but she would not let go.

*

Before 'opening up', Chinese people's lives were tied to where the government said they were from. Without a local *hukou* a person couldn't get housing, medical treatment, education or even their quota of food. In the absence of private enterprise people had to play by the rules of the state. But today what matters most in China (like virtually everywhere else) is how much money a person has. Someone who can afford to pay for private healthcare and education for their child, and who has enough money to buy property, doesn't have to worry much about not holding a local *hukou*. The endemic low-level corruption in China means there's usually a way around any difficult regulations, such as those prohibiting non-residents from buying a car or a house. And for some of China's richest people, the ultimate exemption from the requirements of the state is to leave the country completely. A study by the Bank of China found that 60 per cent of the country's richest (those worth more than $1.5 million) were either in the process of moving abroad or thinking about doing so.[11]

Given the rising cost of living in major cities, and the unlikelihood of *hukou* requirements being relaxed for anyone without wealth or a university degree, many rural migrants are likely to end up being forced to move to the peripheries. In most cases their lack of education and training means they can't get better-paying jobs and so are stuck at a low income level. A study by the All-China Federation of Trade Unions found that 60 per cent of urban jobs require senior middle school education levels, which only 30 per cent of younger migrant workers have.[12]

In Shenzhen I spoke to several migrants who foresaw themselves having to leave. One grey-haired woman from Anhui province said she and her husband liked living in Shenzhen, even though she had to make a living by collecting plastic bottles, cans and newspapers she sold to recyclers. She was wearing a bright fuchsia blouse, and as we talked she punctured Coke and Fanta bottles with a long nail. She'd been in Shenzhen since 1999 and didn't have anything good to say about Anhui. 'All we used to eat there was steamed bread.' The problem was that her rent had gone up 20 per cent in the last year.

'What happens if it goes up more?'

She shrugged. 'We will go back.'

Though for the immediate future the urban villages of Shenzhen are likely to provide affordable accommodation for most migrants, development within its central districts continues, which will inevitably push up rents. This isn't likely to be stopped by the fact that Shenzhen is very short of land, and not just for building new properties.[13] There's also a lack of places to put construction waste. In December 2015 a huge landslide destroyed 33 buildings and killed at least 60 people.[14] The cause was neither an earthquake nor heavy rain, but that a man-made waste pile was too large. The mound was mostly formed of construction dirt, and was only supposed to be stored at its site temporarily. A number of safety warnings had been issued, all of which were ignored.

In Futian district I went to one of the city's last remaining *danwei*, which was being redeveloped into a set of luxury apartments called Dong Mountain Compound. One of the old tenement blocks had already been reduced to rubble, while another building had been vacated. But there were still several inhabited buildings, on each of which there was a long orange banner with a message from the developer, Kaisa Group, one of Shenzhen's biggest property companies. 'Kaisa sincerely thanks each home owner for their support and cooperation. We wish to have great success in collecting houses!' said one of them. On the edge of the rubble there was a basketball court on which a small group of young men were playing. They were watched by a man with thinning hair in shorts and sandals sitting in an office chair. I asked him when the other tenants would have to move out. 'No idea,' he said without taking his eyes off the players.

An elderly woman pushing a rubbish cart round the compound didn't know either. She'd come from Hubei province the year before to help take care of her grandson while his parents worked. 'I didn't want to be a burden on the family, so I got this job. When the people leave these buildings I'll also probably have to go. But I'll work as long as I can.'

Once started, the demolition process is generally unstoppable – all nail houses eventually get removed – but in the case of Dong Mountain there was a reprieve six months later. Though Kaisa was a fairly successful developer, with rising sales and a listing on the Hong Kong stock exchange, in late 2014 it quickly fell apart. Officials blocked its new projects and property sales and launched an investigation into the company. The measures were linked to a corruption investigation into Jiang Zunyu, who had been in charge of Shenzhen's police, courts and security bureau. The two were connected because Jiang had been Communist Party Secretary in the Longgang district, where many of Kaisa's projects were located, and as one lawyer told the *Financial Times*, 'It is just a fact that property deals in China rely on close collaboration between wealthy property developers and poorly paid officials who have all the power and control all the land [...] Corruption is endemic in real estate.'[15] However, it's worth pointing out that this is more a feature of property development per se than something particular to China. Property developers in cities from London to Sydney frequently execute sales transactions involving shell corporations, while public officials in many countries obtain bribes from people seeking permits. Corruption in property development is just another way in which most of the problems faced by China's cities are the same as those facing cities all over the world.

Kaisa's woes continued. A year later it become the first Chinese property developer to default on its overseas debt of around $2.5 billion, money it had borrowed to pay for land purchases. In January 2016 the ban was lifted on sales in order to help Kaisa deal with its debts.

The company's problems illustrate some of the ways in which corruption runs through China's political and financial spheres, but also points to some of the contradictions in the notion of the Chinese Dream, at least as it is articulated at an official level. China's cities rely on property development to finance themselves, but if the Communist Party is truly serious about abolishing corruption, it's likely to be ruinous for both local governments and the property development sector. From this perspective, the Chinese government will have to choose between competing dreams: one based on prosperity and one based on principle.

9

EVERY CARP REQUIRES GOOD FORTUNE

The Foton Motor factory in Changsha is a place of worship. The object of reverence is not the trucks and tractors made by the company, nor even the organisation itself. In the entrance hall there are no statues of Buddha, no lions, tigers, dragons or any other bringers of fortune. There is no altar or smell of incense, just a single photo blown up to fill an entire wall. In it five Foton executives wearing white shirts and dark trousers watch another identically dressed man shake the hand of Xi Jinping, who is smiling his most avuncular smile while wearing a light-blue shirt whose non-whiteness seems to emphasise his imperial status.

Foton has many reasons to celebrate the blessings of its links with the president. The company is a subsidiary of the state-owned BAIC group, which makes a variety of machines and automobiles; Foton specialises in tractors, vans, buses and trucks, a third of which are for export. Xi Jinping has done a lot more for Foton than just being part of a photo opportunity. During a visit to India in 2015 he signed an agreement for the creation of a new Foton industrial plant and supplier park worth $300 million, one of China's biggest investments in India.[1]

Though Foton has factories in a number of coastal provinces, it's well represented in inland provinces like Hunan and Hubei, mainly because it focuses on the domestic market. But in recent years this has also meant it's been better placed to deal with an issue many never

CHASING THE CHINESE DREAM

expected to come across in China: a shortage of workers. Since the financial crisis in 2008, when many workers lost their jobs in coastal factories and had to return to their home provinces, the number of migrants travelling far in search of work has declined (though in many provinces this is still around half the people of working age). Rising salaries for workers – partly due to general inflation, most notably in the price of food, though also due to labour activism – have caused the wage gap between the coast and the interior to narrow. After taking into account the costs of transportation and higher living expenses in places like Beijing and Guangzhou, more and more workers are opting to find work closer to home, and thus their families. China hasn't yet reached the end of surplus labour from the countryside – what economists call the Lewis Turning Point – but some analysts think this is likely to occur between 2020 and 2025.

This shift in migration patterns has major implications for the growth of small and medium-sized Chinese cities in the interior. Rural migrants who go to these places to find work may end up becoming urban citizens (assuming the local *hukou* system permits), and thus may also buy property there. If this happens, it's likely to reduce the number of families who have to be torn apart by the need for the parents to work so far from home. Even if their kids can't go to the school in that city, at least they'll be close enough to their home towns to make it possible for them to return at weekends. The caveat for all this is that it depends on the Chinese economy remaining strong enough to generate enough new jobs in these places, something that looks uncertain at the time of writing: in January 2016 the Chinese stock market crashed multiple times and its economy was growing at its slowest rate for 25 years.

The Foton factory in Changsha employs around 2,000 people. When I went to speak to one of its managers, Mr Yan, about whether they had a labour shortage, he had a more pressing question for me. Leaning back in his leather chair, he asked what I thought of the women of Shaoyang.

'I don't know,' I said quite truthfully.

'Shaoyang girls love to fight!' he said. 'But Changsha girls are tougher.' He nodded with pride, then held up a hand as if to forestall my objection. 'But the best girls are from Sichuan province. They are not possessive.' He smiled broadly, leaned back further, then drank water from a plastic cup embossed with the company logo. I endeavoured to return to the topic by asking where most of their employees came from.

Mr Yan's reply was less enthusiastic. 'Most of our workers come from the countryside, maybe about 60 per cent from outside Hunan. About two-thirds of them are under 30. There are some technical schools in the area that help with recruitment, but there is a big worker turnover. In the first quarter of this year 20 per cent of our workers left.'

'Is that normal?'

He shrugged. 'Now it is. January to April is our busy season, when they have to work ten-hour days at least and only have two days off per month. But the wages are good. They get between 3,500 and 4,000 yuan, an increase of 15 per cent since last year.'

'Why do so many leave?'

'They get tired or bored after six months. Young men don't want to work so much – they are only working because of pressure from their parents. If we criticise a worker's performance, he says, "Fire me! I don't want to work. My mum pushed me to work so I could get a cell phone. Now I have one, I want to quit."' He shook his head. 'Really, I wish we could replace them with robots.'

Mr Yan was possibly joking, but a major automation push is under way in south China. The three largest cities in Guangdong province offer subsidies of between 200 and 500 million yuan to factories that install robots on their assembly lines,[2] while Foxconn has announced plans to have 30 per cent of its labour automated in China by 2020. In May 2015 construction began in Dongguan of China's first factory to use only robots.

Mr Yan had arranged for me to talk to some of the factory's workers. I'd assumed I'd be speaking to them in a canteen or meeting room, but instead we had to talk in their boss's office. Four of them, wearing blue overalls, shared the same expressions of bafflement about being called to speak to a random foreigner. If I'd been able to speak to them on my own, I might have put them at ease, but in front of Mr Yan our conversation was an exercise in awkwardness. They didn't mind saying where they came from (three from Hunan, one from Guangxi) or that they'd been working in the factory for between nine months and three years. But it was difficult to ask them how they felt about their job in front of their boss. Two of them said they had originally gone together to a factory in Guangzhou, but had come back to Hunan to find work because they didn't like how they were treated. Even this elicited nervous glances from the other two workers, and provoked an interruption from Mr Yan. Like Da Ming in Guangzhou four years before, Mr Yan felt the need to defend the honour of factory managers. 'Bosses are under a lot of pressure,' he said. 'They always have a boss too.'

After fifteen minutes, I admitted defeat and thanked Mr Yan and the workers for their time. I was sure I'd have better luck when I went back to Da Ming's factory in Guangzhou. He and I were old friends, and I didn't think he'd mind me talking to the workers without him being present. When I remembered that factory I thought of its guard dog, and his mother and father working there as well. It would be good to see him again.

*

Da Ming would probably have let me talk to his workers; the problem was that he no longer had a factory. In 2011 the global financial crash had ruined him. Da Ming had been forced by the massive drop in international orders to fold his business. He ended up selling the machinery for almost nothing. 'I went from ten million yuan to being almost broke in six months,' he told me matter-of-factly.

We were speaking in the considerably reduced circumstances of his new premises in Baiyun district in northern Guangzhou. Instead of the three-floor building overlooking the fields, he had a dingy ground floor partitioned into two offices and a workshop. There was no thrum of sewing machines, no sounds of leather being drilled, stamped and flattened. There were just four people sitting round a table under fluorescent lights. They were folding, packing and sealing, slipping pouches and wallets and mobile-phone protectors into cellophane sleeves and blister packs. He'd managed to hold on to a few of his clients, but now he was only a distributor. 'Some of my customers were very loyal,' he said. 'But I learnt that in business you have to hide that you are broken. Many people said they could not wait three months for me to reorganise my company.'

Some things hadn't changed. I recognised his assistant, a thin young woman who wore her hair in a braid and had a cheeky face. She was wearing a T-shirt on which it said, in English, 'I WILL NEVER BE LIKE YOUR KING OF THE GIRLS'. She looked up from her work, showed all her teeth in a smile, then went back to sliding strips of card into cellophane. There was also still the factory dog who wandered like a shadow between rooms.

While the basic goal of the Chinese Dream – to develop China into a moderately prosperous society through mass urbanisation – is feasible, its achievement within the near future depends on factors beyond the Chinese government's control. The vicissitudes of global markets are obviously one, to which might be added the future impacts of climate change and the health (and financial) costs of China's environmental pollution. Da Ming (and many like him) had worked hard for a decade to build an apparently solid business, then lost it due to forces that seem to many to be as implacable as the weather. Though he did not seem bitter or disheartened by his losses, the experience had made him consider how he might stop the same thing happening again. After the crash he had sought some feng shui advice, and had obviously taken it seriously. In the foyer there was a fish tank, an altar dusted with incense and a cluster of golden tiles on the wall. Above the door there was a framed calligraphy scroll that said, 'Hard work always brings rewards'. All he needed was a photo of Xi Jinping.

I asked what the golden tiles were for.

'They are to reflect good fortune.'

Da Ming's new premises were located in a side street of Jianggao, a subdistrict of Baiyun. Like a lot of factory towns in south China, it had been constructed with only utility in mind. The streets were unsurfaced concrete, most of which were laid out according to a grid except for where a natural feature or existing building had been too big or difficult to remove. I saw no parks or playgrounds; there were no trees on the streets.

Ten years ago much of the area had been farmland, but as rents went up in Guangzhou, many smaller businesses had been pushed farther out of the city. The services of Jianggao had yet to catch up with the quick rise in its population. Many of its shops were orientated to the needs of local enterprises rather than those of ordinary consumers. The main street was a lesson in single-commodity capitalism. One shop sold nothing except nails; its neighbour had plastic tubing, the next ceramic tiles. There was a shop for engine batteries, ones for metal piping, fire extinguishers, sinks. There was a room where an old man wearing thick glasses sat on a chair and read a newspaper, surrounded only by eggs. You could easily buy a spade or drill or new car tyres, but I saw nowhere to buy a TV, lamp or pair of curtains, anything you might want to make the place you lived in more comfortable. Most of the people living there were from somewhere else, and would probably go back there. They didn't need to buy ornaments.

At lunchtime Da Ming and I ordered dumplings in a small restaurant. While we waited for them to cook we ate cold cucumber with raw garlic.

'How is it?' he said.

'It's perfect.'

'Nick, I think you are very used to Chinese food by now. But not all foreigners are. Some of my American clients are frightened of the chilli pepper.'

'Do you still have many of those clients?'

'I have one company, where my friends David, Brenda and Adam work. Last year I visited them in North Dakota.'

'Did you like it?' I asked, remembering how much he'd disliked his previous trips to Europe.

'It's great. We went ice fishing and had a very good time.'

'Have you been anywhere else?'

'I went to see a client in Germany. They offered to take me to Karl Marx's birthplace, but I thought it was useless. I wanted to see the BMW factory instead.'

The dumplings arrived. As I was reaching for the vinegar he said, 'There has been a lot of trouble for me, but now I think it will be better. My wife is expecting another child.'

'That's good. But will it be a problem because it's your second?'

'Maybe we must pay a big fine. I don't care about that. But maybe my wife will go to Hunan to have it. If she is fined there, it will be cheaper.'

In terms of timing, he was unlucky: 18 months later, in November 2015, the Chinese government announced the end of the one-child policy.[3] This isn't the end of family-planning laws in China: parents who have more than two children will still face fines and harassment, and unmarried women will still be denied a 'reproduction permit'. But it will certainly save some parents money and trouble, and may help to rebalance the sex ratio in China, which has become heavily skewed towards males: in 2004, for every 100 girls born in China there were 121 boys.

Even though Da Ming's child would probably cause him to incur a large fine, in another respect he and his wife were fortunate. She had a Guangzhou *hukou*, which meant her son or daughter could have one too. The child would thus be able to go to public school in Guangzhou, and be eligible for health and welfare benefits. Given that he'd already brought his parents to live in the city, it meant that his family now had few ties to the countryside. You could argue that in the space of a single generation his whole family had achieved the Chinese Dream, but whose dream was it? Da Ming's parents hadn't wanted to come and live in the city at all.

After lunch I went to try to find some part of Jianggao that hadn't been built in the last decade. This was always my task whenever I went anywhere new. To some degree this was due to an interest in Chinese history, though I don't rule out the possibility that some quasi-Orientalist notion about old wooden houses being more authentically Chinese than 30-storey apartment blocks was often at work. But my strongest motivation was a sense of the precariousness of China's visible history, how it was usually imperilled by the pursuit of money or modernity. A structure that had stood for several hundred years could vanish in an afternoon. In a place like Jianggao (or Shaoyang) such losses would barely be noticed, and probably quickly forgotten.

There's no sure-fire way to find the older parts of an unfamiliar place, but getting far away from the larger roads is usually a good start. On the main street in Jianggao the houses were packed tightly for three or four rows on either side, and had probably been built around the same time as the road. If you were driving through you might think Jianggao was a fairly substantial town. But it was like the facade of a Wild West settlement; behind the four-storey buildings the ground sloped down to an open space of small fields and lush vegetation. There the presence of the city was limited to an abandoned sofa and a pile of antibiotics someone had tried to burn.

Between the fields and the apartment blocks there was still a single layer of small brick houses, many of which had vertical strips of red paper asking for good fortune and health pasted either side of their wooden doors. A narrow road curved up through these back towards the main street. By the side of it, against a brick wall, porcelain figurines clustered round a headstone. The woman had died in 1999, but the grave was well tended. Seven statues of the goddess Guanyin watched over it, five of them weather-faded but two in which she was resplendent, robed in gold, enthroned on a lotus flower. Were this not protection enough, there was also both a framed portrait and a large painted figurine of Guan Yu, the red-faced, long-bearded guardian deity who manages to simultaneously be a historical figure (a general during the Eastern Han dynasty), a literary character (in the classic *Romance of the Three Kingdoms*) and the subject of worship in three different (albeit overlapping) religions: Confucianism, Daoism and Chinese Buddhism.

Though Guan Yu only played a supporting role at the grave, he was the star of a grey stone temple further down the road. There his incarnation was a large gold figure perched on a red throne. The offerings before him were meagre: four apples, some tangerines and a large ripe pomelo. But there were other signs of devotion. A thicket of red incense stubs filled a large iron trough, while the floor was so stained by firecracker paper it had a pink blush.

Outside, a line of grey-haired women sat on a long stone bench in the shade of an awning. Slightly apart from them, an old man with a passing resemblance to Samuel Beckett smoked the stub of a cigarette. The afternoon was hot and their plastic sandals dangled loosely from their feet. We spoke for a few minutes about obvious things – the heat, my foreignness – then I asked one of the women what she thought of all the changes in Jianggao.

'Which changes?' she said.

'The new buildings. The factories.'

She made a slow noise of comprehension, then said, 'Yes, there are a lot of those.'

'She's right,' said Beckett.

Several other women nodded, as if her answer was all that needed to be said. When I asked the woman a follow-up question, all she did was smile then adjust her jade bracelet.

As I walked away I wondered, not for the first time, how people felt about having a random foreigner ask them what they thought about the state of their nation. While issues like urbanisation and China's future development have some relevance for (and impact on) everyone in the country, whether they are in Beijing, Guangzhou or rural Hunan, I guessed that very few people were sitting around talking about what the 'Chinese Dream' meant to them. They might see the slogan on a poster, or hear it on TV, but for most people it would remain abstract. The significant changes would be those that happened locally, whether it was the building of a new road or train station, the demolition of houses or the seizure of land they and their families had worked for decades. On a personal level it might mean a parent being able to send their child to school in the same city where they lived, being able to see their son or daughter not just several times a year, but every day. It could mean the death of villages like Weiping's, the rejuvenation of towns like Shaoyang.

When I got back to the office later that afternoon the dog was barking viciously. 'I don't know what he is saying,' said Da Ming. 'He has gone crazy.'

His assistant came in to give him a message, and she wasn't smiling. Da Ming listened while making low-pitched sounds of acknowledgement. Both looked worried.

'Is everything alright?' I asked.

'Another headache problem.'

'Do you want to talk about it?'

'Not now,' he said and left the room. He was gone for an hour, and I felt that I had come at a bad time.

When Da Ming returned, he asked where I'd gone after lunch. I told him about the temple and the old people's club, which were only a 20-minute walk from the office.

'I don't know about that place. And I have been here three years now! All I do is stay in this office. Maybe I should be an employee again. Then I would not have to worry about all the things.'

He sounded defeated. For the next half-hour we sat in the office not talking, staring at our phones and our laptops. Then he shut his laptop a little harder than was probably necessary.

'Nick, are you busy?'

I wasn't.

'Shall we go for a foot massage?'

'Yeah. Do you want to go to those ones round the corner?'

'We cannot. We must drive to another district.'

'Why?'

'All the ones here are places for sex. It would not be good to go there. I have some friends who I do business with who go to those places, but I never do that. I remember what you told us about the AIDS.'

During my last term in Shaoyang I had attempted to teach sex education to my final-year students (most of whom were 21). They'd had little or no formal education about it previously, and were very shy about the topic. When I drew a condom on the blackboard, most of them fixed their eyes on the ground, except for one girl who stared and smiled without blinking. At the end I gave them all a piece of paper and told them to write either a question or something they had learned, so that it wouldn't be obvious who had asked a question. Most of the responses were sensible questions or comments like 'We have never had a lesson like this before. We are girls and feel shy. But thank you.'

Not all of the responses were positive. One person wrote, 'If everyone leads a normal and healthy life, I think HIV and AIDS are far away from us. So it's none of my business.' But I was glad I'd done the lesson, and hoped it could help them make informed choices. As we walked to the car, almost fifteen years later, Da Ming said that knowing that a condom didn't always work had made him very careful.

171

'Before I met my wife I was not a playboy. I only had one serious girlfriend at Shaoyang.'

'What happened to her?'

'After graduation she left me.'

'Are you in contact with her?'

'No,' he said, and there was a flash of old anger. 'But I am sure she isn't doing as well as me.'

We drove to Huadu, a neighbouring district, and had an accident on the way. The driver in front braked for no apparent reason and although we were several car lengths behind, we could not stop in time. There wasn't much damage to Da Ming's car, just scratched paintwork and a bent bumper. The problem was that the other driver claimed it wasn't his car, and that he had no licence. 'I must call the owner,' he said, but didn't seem in a rush to do so. Da Ming thought the man was pretending not to own the car to try and avoid having to pay for the damage, but didn't know what else to do except take the man's registration and phone number. He got back in the car and said, 'This is a wonderful game, but I don't have time to enjoy it.'

The massage parlour did its best to make its clients feel like VIPs. We were greeted by girls in long red dresses wearing sashes that made them look like beauty pageant winners. Red-carpeted stairs led to a first-floor seating area bathed in pink light. But there was nothing sleazy about the place, and our massage was anything but sensual. The two young women who massaged us had very hard hands. They were both from Hengyang in Hunan and were soon laughing and talking with Da Ming in a dialect I couldn't follow. The high point was when they used a hard plastic comb on his back that brought up long red welts like claw marks.

'You should see the state of your back,' I said.

'Don't worry,' he said. 'It's very good for the health.'

I lay back and watched them scratch him more. Even the two masseuses were amazed by how red his back became; it seemed about to bleed.

Afterwards, as the light was fading, we walked slowly round a miniature version of the Meixi Lake development. The luxury apartments were only 20 storeys high; the lake was ten inches deep. But it was still an open space with trees and grass and few people in sight. On one side of the lake the only building visible was a derelict cement factory that looked like a haunted castle. It would have been wonderful to explore, but unfortunately I got caught by the nightwatchman while climbing over a wall. The man was bald and had a chained-up dog that looked very bored. He and I had a friendly chat for several minutes, at the end of which I was still not permitted to trespass.

The back scraping had relaxed Da Ming to the point that he seemed subdued.

'It's nice here,' I said. 'You should walk here more often.'

'Maybe in 20 years I will have time to read a book here. I have too many headache problems now.'

I suggested that things weren't so bad, at least compared to 2011. He just shook his head.

On the drive back I thought about my male students in Shaoyang, 15 years before, saying they wanted to be businessmen. They'd never studied business or economics, had no experience of it, and had no idea what kind of business they might go into. It was just a path to money and status that was suddenly possible. Despite his recent setbacks Da Ming had done amazingly well. Like Wenli in Shanghai, he'd swum to the top of the waterfall; the problem was that no matter how hard you swam, sometimes you slipped back down.

When we got back to the office Da Ming went to a small wooden cabinet in the corner. I hadn't looked inside, assuming it contained commercial samples like the other display cases on the premises. But instead of a pouch or phone case, he took out two brown ceramic cups. He put them on a low table, then cleared enough room for him to put a small black tray on it.

'Let's have some tea,' he said. The tray had grooves for drainage; at one end of it there was a small creature. It had the head of a dragon, and perhaps the body of a lion.

'What's that?'

'It is *Pixiu*. The son of a dragon. It is there for luck.'

In Chinese mythology, *Pixiu* is said to have had an insatiable appetite for gold. When *Pixiu* angered the Jade Emperor (the supreme god in Daoism), it was punished by having its bowels sealed to prevent it expelling the gold. As a result, *Pixiu* is associated with both acquiring and keeping wealth, an idea that obviously resonated with Da Ming.

But it's not enough to just have a *Pixiu* – it must be taken care of. When the water was hot, Da Ming poured some over the cups, the tea board, and the *Pixiu*.

'If you wash it a lot the colour will change. And its powers depend on the colour. I have only had this *Pixiu* for two years, so it hasn't changed much.'

Most *Pixiu* are made of rough clay – with repeated washing they become shinier and also absorb the aroma of the tea used. Da Ming's favourite was a pale green tea from Fujian province with a light, refreshing flavour. He admitted that it was expensive, but said it was the only thing he liked to spend money on.

'This is a good thing about the export business. My friend sells hospital machines, and he must always be taking hospital administrators and doctors out for dinner and for drinking. But I don't like that, it is no good.'

He nodded in emphasis, then picked up a small brush. 'You must do this every time,' he said, smoothing the tea into the head and back of the *Pixiu*. He did it slowly, with care, wholly absorbed in the task. He still believed that luck was possible.

EPILOGUE

THE ART OF THE POSSIBLE

When I first went to live in China, the one question all my friends and relatives asked me was 'What's China like?' Most had never visited the country, and had no Chinese friends. But all of them had ideas about the place. Some thought China must be fascinating and strange, while others viewed the country as a tightly controlled society rife with inequality and human rights violations. Some thought both of these things. It was a fair question, and one I should have been able to answer, but I always struggled with it. If they'd asked me what Shaoyang was like, I could have told them, but to say anything definitive about so vast a country with such variation in geography, cuisine and culture seemed not only foolish but wrong, even after three years of living and travelling extensively in China.

Fifteen years later, I still find it hard to make pronouncements about the state of the country, let alone its future, which puts me in a tricky position given that the customary thing to do at the end of a book such as this is to offer some prognosis, in this case to issue a verdict on the viability of the 'Chinese Dream'. Mercifully, the notion is so amorphous, and with so few measurable goals, that I can weasel my way out of having to give an answer as to whether the 'national rejuvenation' proposed by Xi Jinping is likely to occur, or how successful the government is likely to be in its efforts towards the 'construction of a better society'. Both, I suspect, are likely to be a matter of perspective.

One facet of the Chinese Dream that can be quantified is its commitment to increasing the proportion of the population living in cities. Even if the goal of having 70 per cent of the population living in urban centres by 2025 isn't achieved, it seems safe to say that the proportion won't be far off. The next generation of young people are unlikely to have any strong connection with the land; most will grow up in large towns and small cities, and will probably only spend time in the countryside when they go to visit their grandparents (many of whom would have been part of that first wave of migrant workers in the 1980s). Fengyan's children won't be able to plant or harvest rice; Weiping's won't know which kind of grass to cut for the water buffalo. China's middle class, once detached from their rural origins, might start to view the countryside as a place of leisure, somewhere to hike and ramble at weekends, especially since all the major cities are likely to remain severely polluted for the next few decades.

Whether or not the *hukou* system survives in its present form is another matter. At the time of writing, if one has enough money and connections, one's *hukou* status doesn't pose a problem. In China, as elsewhere, the gap between the haves and have nots is widening fast. But this is not to say that people without either money or *guanxi* are helpless in the face of what amounts to a system of apartheid. Every migrant worker in China is attempting, in some fashion, to overcome the social and institutional boundaries the system seeks to impose. Though there have arguably been periods of China's recent history when many people had to say *mei ban fa* and just try to endure awful, unfair conditions, such as during the Cultural Revolution, in my experience most people in China are just as determined to achieve their dreams as people in countries with more permissive governments.

To some the notion of 'achieving one's dreams' may seem childish, a way of talking and thinking that doesn't square with the complexities and constraints of adult life. I confess that I thought that way about some of my students' aspirations, given the obstacles facing them as the sons and daughters of far from prosperous parents, not to mention their presence at a second-rate institution like Shaoyang Teachers' College. Even for bright or well-connected students, the barriers were high.

But in spite of this some of my students did succeed, mainly through sheer persistence and a belief in their own abilities. Both Da Ming in Guangzhou and Wenli in Shanghai, and to some degree Xiao Long as well, were testament to the fact that even though inequality has grown rapidly in Chinese society since 1979, for their generation there were also possibilities that didn't exist before. What they (and many of the other people I met) had in common was a powerful combination of ambition and pragmatism, a refusal to say *mei ban fa* when faced with social and institutional barriers. Though they faced hardship in many guises – losing their jobs or their business, having to leave their homes – and were often constrained by their duties to their relatives, most were still working towards the realisation of some version of their ambitions. Some, like Xiao Long and Da Ming, had been forced to change their dreams to fit what was possible, but they were still swimming against the current. They were going to keep trying to climb the waterfall.

ACKNOWLEDGEMENTS

This book began while I was working at *chinadialogue*, during which time I learnt a great deal about environmental issues in China. I'm grateful to my colleagues Isabel Hilton, Sam Geall, Tom Levitt, Olivia Boyd, Lushan Huang, Beth Walker, Jessica Jacoby and Abigail Coombs for providing such a stimulating working environment.

I'm also indebted to the excellent editors who worked on some of the material included in this book, especially Brendan Barrington, who edits the *Dublin Review*, and Thomas Jones, who edits the *London Review of Books* blog.

This book would also not have been possible without the help of Joyce Du and Ding Tan, both of whom helped me make invaluable contacts.

I'd also like to thank Creative Scotland, who helped fund several of my trips to China.

NOTES

INTRODUCTION – BIG CITY DREAMS

1 George Pearson, *Get Up and Go: The Autobiography of a Medical Missionary* (London: Epworth Press, 1968), p. 49.

2 *Xinhua*, 'Transport to be fully stretched for "Chunyun"', China.org.cn (14 January 2014). Available at http://www.china.org.cn/china/2014-01/14/content_31193069.htm.

3 David Pierson, 'Unable to get train ticket, man strips in frustration, becomes Chinese internet sensation', *Los Angeles Times* (24 January 2011). Available at http://latimesblogs.latimes.com/money_co/2011/01/unable-to-get-train-ticket-man-strips-in-frustration-becomes-chinese-internet-sensation.html.

4 Tom Miller, *China's Urban Billion: The Story Behind the Biggest Migration in Human History* (London: Zed Books, 2012).

5 Li Keqiang, 'Releasing growth potential', *China Daily USA* (20 Feb 2012). Available at http://usa.chinadaily.com.cn/business/2012-02/20/content_14649453.htm.

6 CCTV.com [website], 'China to work towards achieving national rejuvenation' (3 April 2014). Available at http://english.cntv.cn/program/china24/20140304/105384.shtml.

7 Ian Johnson, 'Old dreams for a new China', *New York Review of Books* [website] (15 October 2013). Available at http://www.nybooks.com/daily/2013/10/15/china-dream-posters/.

8 Ian Johnson, 'A Chinese folk artist's descendants are split by the government's use of their family legacy', *New York Times* (5 December 2015). Available at http://www.nytimes.com/2015/12/06/world/asia/a-chinese-folk-artists-descendants-are-split-by-the-governments-use-of-their-family-legacy.html?ref=world&_r=3.

9 'Moving on up', *The Economist* (22 March 2014). Available at http://www.economist.com/news/china/21599397-government-unveils-new-people-centred-plan-urbanisation-moving-up.

10   Adam Vaughan, 'City dwellers have smaller carbon footprint, study finds',
     Guardian (23 March 2009). Available at https://www.theguardian.com/
     environment/2009/mar/23/city-dwellers-smaller-carbon-footprints.

1 JUMPING THE DRAGON GATE

1   James T. Areddy, 'Shanghai's Pudong, once soulless, rises up', *Wall
     Street Journal* (21 December 2011). Available to subscribers at http://
     www.wsj.com/news/articles/SB1000142405297020477040457708049
     1863427170?mg=reno64-wsj&url=http%3A%2F%2Fonline.wsj.com
     %2Farticle%2FSB10001424052970204770404577080491863427170.
     html.
2   Tom Miller, 'Time for a reality check on China's ghost cities', *chinadialogue*
     [website] (8 October 2013). Available at https://www.chinadialogue.
     net/article/show/single/en/6402-Time-for-a-reality-check-on-China-
     s-ghost-cities.
3   Trish Saywell, 'Pudong rises to the task', *Far Eastern Economic Review*
     163 (44) (2 November 2000).
4   Wade Shepard, 'Nanhui, China's unbelievable ghost city on the coast',
     Vagabond Journey [blog] (20 June 2014). Available at http://www.
     vagabondjourney.com/nanhui-ghost-city-china/.
5   Han Heng, 'University graduates from the countryside drifting in the
     City', *Chinese Sociology and Anthropology* 43 (1) (Fall 2010), pp. 42–65.
6   Ibid.
7   Tania Branigan, 'Shanghai Expo 2010: tight security as city prepares
     for opening', *Guardian* (30 April 2010). http://www.theguardian.com/
     world/2010/apr/30/shanghai-world-expo-2010-launch.
8   Wade Shepard, *Ghost Cities of China* (London: Zed Books, 2015),
     p. 33.
9   Luo Ruiyao, 'China's Cities "Not Telling Public about Debt Levels"',
     Caixin (6 August 2015). Available to subscribers at http://english.
     caixin.com/2015-08-06/100837111.html.
10   'China 2030: building a modern, harmonious, and creative society'. Available
     at http://documents.worldbank.org/curated/en/781101468239669951/
     pdf/762990PUB0china0Box374372B00PUBLIC0.pdf.
11   Martin Patience, 'China's Wukan village stands up for land rights', *BBC
     News* [website] (15 December 2011). Available at http://www.bbc.co.uk/
     news/world-asia-china-16205654.

12 Frank Langfitt, 'Desperate Chinese villagers turn to self-immolation', *NPR* [website] (23 October 2013). Available at http://www.npr.org/sections/parallels/2013/10/23/239270737/desperate-chinese-villagers-turn-to-self-immolation.

13 Ian Johnson, 'Picking death over eviction', *New York Times* (8 September 2013). Available at http://www.nytimes.com/2013/09/09/world/asia/as-chinese-farmers-fight-for-homes-suicide-is-ultimate-protest; 'Twelve Chinese petitioners in pesticide suicide bid', *Radio Free Asia* [website] (16 July 2014). Available at http://www.rfa.org/english/news/china/suicide-07162014143830.html.

2 BUTTERING THE TIGER

1 David Barboza, 'In Chinese factories, lost fingers and low pay', *New York Times* (5 January 2008). Available at http://www.nytimes.com/2008/01/05/business/worldbusiness/05sweatshop.html.

2 Tania Branigan, 'Chinese state steel workers beat private firm boss to death', *Guardian* (26 July 2009). Available at http://www.theguardian.com/world/2009/jul/26/china-steel-workers-riot.

3 William Hurst, 'Slowdown in the world's workshop?: Chinese labor and the global recession', in Dali L. Yang (ed.), *The Global Recession and China's Political Economy (China in Transformation)* (New York: Palgrave Macmillan, 2012), pp. 117–30.

4 Malcolm Moore, '"Mass suicide" protest at Apple manufacturer Foxconn factory', *Telegraph* (11 January 2012). Available at http://www.telegraph.co.uk/news/worldnews/asia/china/9006988/Mass-suicide-protest-at-Apple-manufacturer-Foxconn-factory.html.

5 Erik Kain, 'Conditions at Apple iPad plants better than average, according to Fair Labor Association', *Forbes* (15 February 2012). Available at http://www.forbes.com/sites/erikkain/2012/02/15/conditions-at-apple-ipad-plants-better-than-average-according-to-fair-labor-association/.

3 THE MANY TRIALS OF MR HORSE

1 Christopher Carothers, 'China's divorce rate crosses new threshold', *Wall Street Journal* [blog] (June 18 2010). Available at http://blogs.wsj.com/chinarealtime/2010/06/18/china%E2%80%99s-divorce-rate-crosses-new-threshold/.

4 A TWISTED LOVE

1   Alex Brown and Mitchell Murphy, 'Beijing's perfect opening', *Sydney Morning Herald* (8 August 2008). Available at http://www.smh.com.au/news/off-the-field/beijings-perfect-opening/2008/08/08/1218139087755.html.

2   Edward Wong, '"Airpocalypse" smog hits Beijing at dangerous levels', *New York Times* (*Sinosphere*) [website] (16 January 2014). Available at http://sinosphere.blogs.nytimes.com/2014/01/16/airpocalypse-smog-hits-beijing-at-dangerous-levels/?_r=0.

3   e.g. 'Beijing's first-ever smog "red alert", in pictures', *Telegraph* (5 August 2014). Available at http://www.telegraph.co.uk/news/worldnews/asia/china/12039552/Beijings-first-ever-smog-red-alert-in-pictures.html?frame=3521175.

4   Liu Qin, 'A prayer for clear air', *chinadialogue* (27 February 2014). Available at https://www.chinadialogue.net/books/6769-A-prayer-for-clear-air/en.

5   Steven Q. Andrews, 'China's air pollution reporting is misleading', *chinadialogue* (27 March 2014). Available at https://www.chinadialogue.net/article/show/single/en/6856-China-s-air-pollution-reporting-is-misleading.

6   Liu Qin, 'Cars the main culprit for Beijing's smog: govt figures', *chinadialogue* (2 April 2015). Available at https://www.chinadialogue.net/blog/7829-Cars-the-main-culprit-for-Beijing-s-smog-govt-figures/en.

7   'State Council issues action plan on prevention and control of air pollution', Ministry of Environmental Protection (12 September 2013). Available at http://english.mep.gov.cn/News_service/infocus/201309/t20130924_260707.htm.

8   Li Shuo and Lauri Myllyvirta, 'Beijing won't meet WHO air pollution standards until 2030s', *chinadialogue* (5 April 2013). Available at https://www.chinadialogue.net/blog/5870-Beijing-won-t-meet-WHO-air-pollution-standards-until-2-3-s/en.

9   Yuan Ren, 'Surviving Beijing's pollution while pregnant: "I feel like a lab rat"', *Guardian* (7 March 2014). Available at http://www.theguardian.com/environment/blog/2014/mar/07/surviving-bejings-pollutions-pregnant-lab-rat.

10 Oliver Wainwright, 'Inside Beijing's airpocalypse – a city made "almost uninhabitable" by pollution', *Guardian* (16 December 2014). Available at

http://www.theguardian.com/cities/2014/dec/16/beijing-airpocalypse-city-almost-uninhabitable-pollution-china.

11 Xu Nan, 'China's noxious air "as deadly as smoking": study', *chinadialogue* (4 February 2015). Available at https://www.chinadialogue.net/blog/7697-China-s-noxious-air-as-deadly-as-smoking-study/en.

12 Karl Mathiesen, 'Air pollution causes low birth weight, Beijing study shows', *Guardian* (28 April 2015). Available at http://www.theguardian.com/environment/2015/apr/28/air-pollution-causes-low-birth-weight-beijing-study-shows.

13 Xiaoyi Shao and Sue-Lin Wong, 'Big city land-grab sowing seeds of next China property boom', Reuters [news agency] (6 December 2015). Available at http://www.reuters.com/article/us-china-economy-housing-idUSKBN0TP0UM20151206.

14 'Beijing's population tops 19.6 mln, migration key contributor to growth', *Xinhua* (5 May 2011). Available at http://news.xinhuanet.com/english2010/china/2011-05/05/c_13860069.htm.

15 *Forbes* [website], '#62 Zhang Xin & family'. Available at https://www.forbes.com/profile/zhang-xin/.

16 Tange Associates website. Available at http://www.tangeweb.com/staff.php?lang=en.

17 You-Tien Hsing, *The Great Urban Transformation: Politics of Land and Property in China* (Oxford: Oxford University Press, 2011).

18 David Bray, *Social Space and Governance in Urban China: The* Danwei *System from Origins to Reform* (Stanford, CA: Stanford University Press, 2005).

19 Michael Dutton, *Streetlife China* (Cambridge: Cambridge University Press, 1999), p. 50.

20 Esther Feng, 'You say weird, I say beautiful: Xi Jinping's criticism doesn't ruffle Soho China', *Wall Street Journal* [website] (3 November 2014). Available at http://blogs.wsj.com/chinarealtime/2014/11/03/you-say-weird-i-say-beautiful-xi-jinping-criticism-doesnt-ruffle-soho-china/.

21 Robin Visser, *Cities Surround the Countryside* (Durham, NC: Duke University Press, 2010), p. 14.

22 Xu Heqian, 'Capital said to plan moving gov't agencies to outskirts', *Caixin* (15 July 2015). Available to subscribers at http://www.caixinglobal.com/2015-07-15/101012332.html.

23 Xuefei Ren, *Urban China* (Cambridge: Polity Press, 2013), p. 47.

24 Visser, *Cities Surround the Countryside*, p. 13.

25 Ibid., p. 59.

26 Sherley Wetherhold, 'The bicycle as symbol of China's transformation', *The Atlantic* (30 June 2012). Available at http://www.theatlantic.com/international/archive/2012/06/the-bicycle-as-symbol-of-chinas-transformation/259177/.

27 Owen Guo, 'A city choking on cars hopes commuters will return to two wheels', *New York Times* (11 November 2015). Available at http://www.nytimes.com/2015/11/12/world/asia/a-city-choking-on-cars-hopes-commuters-will-return-to-two-wheels.html?_r=0.

28 Sean Gallagher, 'Beijing's urban makeover: the "hutong" destruction', *openDemocracy* [website] (11 June 2006). Available at https://www.opendemocracy.net/arts-photography/hutong_destruction_3632.jsp.

29 'Demolished: forced evictions and the tenants' movement in China', *Human Rights Watch* 16 (4) (March 2004). Available at https://www.hrw.org/reports/2004/china0304/china0304.pdf.

30 Human Rights Watch, 'China: tenant rights advocate arbitrarily jailed' (19 December 2003). Available at https://www.hrw.org/legacy/english/docs/2003/12/18/china6762_txt.htm.

31 Anne Henochowicz, 'Housing activists sentenced for "picking quarrels"', *China Digital Times* [website] (5 November 2015). Available at http://chinadigitaltimes.net/2015/11/housing-activists-sentenced-for-picking-quarrels/.

32 Beijing Cultural Heritage Protection Center [website]. Available at www.bjchp.org.

33 Dan Edwards, 'Meet Mr Preservation: He Shuzhong on saving China's cultural heritage', *The Beijinger* (21 May 2010). Available at http://www.thebeijinger.com/blog/2010/05/21/meet-mr-preservation-he-shuzhong-saving-china-s-cultural-heritage.

34 Ian Johnson and Jason Leow, 'Builder Soho China stumbles in Beijing', *Wall Street Journal* (24 December 2008). Full article available to subscribers at http://www.wsj.com/articles/SB123006399599230901.

35 Dan Edwards, 'Beijingers debate why preservation matters in light of Gulou redevelopment', *The Beijinger* (24 May 2010). Available at http://www.thebeijinger.com/blog/2010/05/24/beijingers-debate-why-preservation-matters-light-gulou-redevelopment.

36 Richard Silk, 'China's *hukou* reform plan starts to take shape', *Wall Street Journal* [website] (4 August 2014). Available at http://blogs.wsj.

com/chinarealtime/2014/08/04/chinas-hukou-reform-plan-starts-to-take-shape/.

37 'Despite policy changes, black market for Beijing residency thrives', *Global Times* (26 August 2014). Available at http://www.globaltimes. cn/content/878291.shtml.

38 Fei-Ling Wang, *Organizing Through Division and Exclusion: China's Hukou System* (Stanford, CA: Stanford University Press, 2005).

39 Ibid., p. 182.

40 Jonathan Ansfield and Sharon LaFraniere, 'Editor is fired after criticizing Chinese registration system', *New York Times* (9 March 2010). Available at http://www.nytimes.com/2010/03/10/world/asia/10china.html.

41 Chen Xin, 'Migrant children more likely to miss out on school', *China Daily USA* (8 August 2012). Available at http://usa.chinadaily.com.cn/ china/2012-08/08/content_15650988.htm.

42 'Migrant schools closed in Chinese capital', *BBC News* [website] (17 August 2011). Available at http://www.bbc.co.uk/news/world-asia-pacific-14556906.

43 Yihan Xiong, 'The broken ladder: why education provides no upward mobility for migrant children in China', *The China Quarterly* 221 (March 2015), pp. 161–84.

5 LEFT BEHIND

1 Zhou Dongxu and Zhao Han, 'Closer look: how a child comes to pen the words "death has been my dream"', *Caixin* (15 June 2015). Available to subscribers at http://www.caixinglobal.com/2015-06-15/101012404. html.

2 Tom Phillips, 'China's Xi Jinping says poverty is "nothing to fear" after pesticide deaths', *Guardian* (19 June 2015). Available at http:// www.theguardian.com/world/2015/jun/19/china-xi-jinping-poverty-pesticide-deaths-four-children-guizhou.

3 'Migrant workers and their children', *China Labour Bulletin* (May 2015). Available at http://www.clb.org.hk/content/migrant-workers-and-their-children.

4 'Homeless children found dead in Bijie trash bin', *South China Morning Post* (18 November 2012). Available at http://www.scmp. com/news/china/article/1085364/homeless-children-found-dead-bijie-trash-bin.

5   Phillips, 'China's Xi Jinping says poverty is "nothing to fear" after pesticide deaths'.

6   Wang Xiaodong and Xu Wei, 'Deaths "expose plight of left-behind children"', *China Daily* (12 June 2015). Available at http://www.chinadaily.com.cn/china/2015-06/12/content_20981227.htm.

7   Ibid.

8   Zhuang Pinghui, '"Left-behind children" found stabbed to death in southern China', *South China Morning Post* (5 August 2015). Available at http://www.scmp.com/news/china/society/article/1846701/left-behind-children-found-stabbed-death-southern-china.

9   Jenny Li and Leo Timm, 'Murder of teacher highlights China's "left behind children"', *Epoch Times* (27 October 2015). Available at http://www.theepochtimes.com/n3/1886286-murder-of-teacher-highlights-chinas-left-behind-children/.

10 'Migrant workers and their children', *China Labour Bulletin* (May 2015). Available at http://www.clb.org.hk/content/migrant-workers-and-their-children.

11 Luo Wangshu, 'Left-behind children vulnerable, says report', *China Daily* (27 October 2015). Available at http://www.chinadaily.com.cn/china/2015-10/27/content_22300433.htm.

12 'Down and out in rural China', *The Economist* (23 August 2014). Available at http://www.economist.com/news/china/21613293-many-teenagers-chinese-countryside-do-not-finish-secondary-school-bodes-ill.

13 'The children of migrant workers in China', *China Labour Bulletin* (8 May 2009). Available at http://www.clb.org.hk/en/content/children-migrant-workers-china-2.

14 Jamil Anderlini, 'Will the wheels come off for hub-and-spoke Chinese mega-city of Wuhan?', *Financial Times* (21 September 2010). Available to subscribers at http://www.ft.com/cms/s/0/ee98e5aa-c50f-11df-b785-00144feab49a.html#axzz42DNxcXKj.

15 Evan Osnos, 'Boss rail', *New Yorker* (22 October 2012). Available at http://www.newyorker.com/magazine/2012/10/22/boss-rail.

16 Wei Zhu, 'China, connected', *Foreign Policy* (10 September 2015). Available at http://foreignpolicy.com/2015/09/10/china-connected-hsr-high-speed-rail-successes-and-failures/.

17 Stuart Schram, *Mao's Road to Power: Revolutionary Writings, 1912–49, Volume 1* (London: Routledge, 1992), p. 57.

18 Nick Holdstock, 'China's big society', *London Review of Books* (11 September 2012). Available at http://www.lrb.co.uk/blog/2012/09/11/nick-holdstock/chinas-big-society/.

19 Fauna, 'Unhappy employee sets Hunan Water Company managers on fire', *chinaSMACK* (27 August 2012). Available at https://www.chinasmack.com/unhappy-employee-sets-hunan-water-company-managers-on-fire.

20 Jonathan Watts, 'Chinese "rocket man" wins record payout over farmland dispute', *Guardian* (9 July 2010). Available at http://www.theguardian.com/world/2010/jul/09/chinese-rocketman-wins-payout.

21 Kevin J. O'Brien and Yanhua Deng, 'The reach of the state: work units, family ties and "harmonious demolition"', *The China Journal* 74 (2015).

22 'Top 10 quotes', *China Daily* (31 December 2009). Available at http://www.chinadaily.com.cn/china/2009-12/31/content_9249158.htm.

23 Hui Chang, 'Forced demolition an inevitable pain in China's urbanization', *Global Times* (17 October 2010). Available at http://www.globaltimes.cn/content/582829.shtml.

6 CUTTING GRASS AND WOOD

1 Zhou Dongxu and Zhao Han, 'Closer look: how a child comes to pen the words "death has been my dream"', *Caixin* (15 June 2015). Available to subscribers at http://www.caixinglobal.com/2015-06-15/101012404.html.

2 Tom Phillips, 'China's villages vanish amid rush for the cities', *Telegraph* (23 November 2013). Available at http://www.telegraph.co.uk/news/worldnews/asia/china/10470077/Chinas-villages-vanish-amid-rush-for-the-cities.html.

3 'Who will feed China: agribusiness or its own farmers? Decisions in Beijing echo around the world', Grain (4 August 2012). Available at https://www.grain.org/es/article/entries/4546-who-will-feed-china-agribusiness-or-its-own-farmers-decisions-in-beijing-echo-around-the-world.

4 'Mao's legacy foundation of Chinese rejuvenation', *Global Times* [website] (25 December 2012). Available at http://www.globaltimes.cn/content/834124.shtml.

5 Tom Phillips, 'Mega-Mao no more as ridiculed golden statue destroyed', *Guardian* (8 January 2016). Available at http://www.theguardian.com/world/2016/jan/08/giant-golden-chairman-mao-statue-destroyed-henan-province?CMP=twt_a-world_b-gdnworld.

6   Lizzie Porter, 'Giant golden statue of Chairman Mao built in China', *Telegraph* (8 January 2016). Available at http://www.telegraph.co.uk/travel/destinations/asia/china/articles/Giant-golden-statue-of-Chairman-Mao-built-in-China/.

7   C. Cindy Fan, 'Settlement intention and split households: findings from a migrant survey in Beijing, China', *The China Review* 11 (2) (2011), pp. 11–42.

8   Richard Silk, 'China's *hukou* reform plan starts to take shape', *Wall Street Journal* [website] (4 August 2014). Available at http://blogs.wsj.com/chinarealtime/2014/08/04/chinas-hukou-reform-plan-starts-to-take-shape/.

9   Yasheng Huang, *Capitalism with Chinese Characteristics: Entrepreneurship and the State* (Cambridge; Cambridge University Press, 2008), pp. 124–9.

7   THE BUBBLE

1   Stephen R. Platt, *Provincial Patriots: the Hunanese and Modern China* (Cambridge, MA: Harvard University Press, 2007), p. 36.

2   Top China Travel. Available at http://www.topchinatravel.com/china-attractions/orange-island-park.htm.

3   Dan Levin, 'In China, cinematic flops suggest fading of an icon', *New York Times* (11 March 2013). Available at http://www.nytimes.com/2013/03/12/world/asia/in-china-unpopular-films-suggest-fading-of-icon.html?_r=0.

4   Richard Bernstein, *China 1945: Mao's Revolution and America's Fateful Choice* (New York: Knopf, 2014), pp. 63–4.

5   Ibid.

6   Joe, 'Changsha old city walls razed for relocation, netizens react', *China Smack* [website] (8 March 2012). Available at http://www.chinasmack.com/2012/pictures/changsha-old-city-walls-razed-for-relocation-netizens-react.html.

7   Simon Rabinovich, 'Changsha plan at heart of China stimulus', *Financial Times* (6 August 2012). Available to subscribers at http://www.ft.com/cms/s/0/3dd79744-dfab-11e1-b81c-00144feab49a.html#axzz3x7tiDOp4.

8   Lucy Luo, 'China's obesity epidemic: teaching children to "eat a rainbow"', *Guardian* (24 November 2015). Available at http://www.theguardian.com/global-development-professionals-network/2015/nov/24/defusing-chinas-childhood-obesity-timebomb.

9   American Heart Association, 'Overweight in children' (5 July 2016).

Available at http://www.heart.org/HEARTORG/HealthyLiving/
HealthyKids/ChildhoodObesity/Overweight-in-Children_CM_304054_
Article.jsp#.WMEViBDB6Xk.

10 Sara Hsu, 'China's healthcare reforms', *The Diplomat* (25 May 2015). Available at http://thediplomat.com/2015/05/chinas-health-care-reforms/.

11 Fanfan Wang, 'China healthcare reform sparks feud between foreign drug firms, hospital', *Wall Street Journal* [website] (18 January 2016). Available at http://blogs.wsj.com/chinarealtime/2016/01/18/china-healthcare-reform-sparks-feud-between-foreign-drug-firms-hospital/.

12 Hunan Cancer Hospital [website]. Available at http://en.hnzlyy.com/.

13 Christopher Beam, 'Under the knife', *New Yorker* (25 August 2014). Available at http://www.newyorker.com/magazine/2014/08/25/under-the-knife (accessed 30 September 2015); 'China's medical malpractice mayhem', *Wilson Quarterly* (Summer 2013). Available at http://wilsonquarterly.com/stories/chinas-medical-malpractice-mayhem/.

14 Beam, 'Under the knife'.

15 Esther Fung, 'China's love for skyscrapers defies growth slowdown', *Wall Street Journal* [website] (21 January 2016). Available at http://blogs.wsj.com/chinarealtime/2016/01/21/chinas-love-for-skyscrapers-defies-growth-slowdown/.

16 Huang Youqin, 'Lack of affordable housing threatens China's urban dream', *chinadialogue* (20 September 2013). Available at https://www.chinadialogue.net/article/show/single/en/6365-Lack-of-affordable-housing-threatens-China-s-urban-dream.

17 Ibid.

18 Gregory M. Stein, *Modern Chinese Real Estate Law* (Surrey: Ashgate, 2013), p. 92.

19 Andy Rothman, 'What next? A China housing crash?', *Financial Times* (12 August 2015). Available to subscribers at http://www.ft.com/cms/s/0/8d3c2752-3b54-11e5-bbd1-b37bc06f590c.html#axzz42DNxcXKj.

20 Gady Epstein, 'The China bubble' (12 October 2009). Available at http://www.forbes.com/forbes/2009/1228/economy-ponzi-debt-peking-china-bubble.html.

21 Wade Shepard, 'From farm to city: check out Changsha's Meixi Lake before the skyscrapers', *Vagabond Journey* [blog] (18 May 2013). Available at http://www.vagabondjourney.com/from-farm-to-city-check-out-changshas-meixi-lake-before-the-skyscrapers/.

22 Esther Fung, 'China seeks a way to fill its empty homes', *Wall Street Journal* [website] (10 December 2015). Available at http://blogs.wsj.com/chinarealtime/2015/12/10/china-seeks-a-way-to-fill-its-empty-homes/?mod=blog_flyover.

8 THE VILLAGE IN THE CITY

1   Tom Miller, 'China's plan to empty the bird cage', *Financial Times* (10 June 2009). Available to subscribers at http://www.ft.com/cms/s/0/4accc3bc-5556-11de-b5d4-00144feabdc0.html#axzz42DNxcXKj.

2   Da Wei David Wang, 'Continuity and change in the urban villages of Shenzhen', *International Journal of China Studies* 4 (2) (2013), pp. 233–56.

3   Ibid.

4   Jonathan Bach, '"They come in peasants and leave citizens": urban villages and the making of Shenzhen, China', *Cultural Anthropology* 25 (3) (2010), pp. 421–58.

5   Fulong Wu, Fangzhu Zhang and Chris Webster (eds), *Rural Migrants in Urban China: Enclaves and Transient Urbanism* (London: Routledge, 2013), p. 263.

6   Ibid.

7   Gary Sigley, 'Metropole power: approaches to centre and periphery in contemporary China', *International Journal of China Studies* 4 (2) (2013), pp. 177–87.

8   Dongping Yang (ed.), *The China Educational Development Yearbook*, vol. 2 (Leiden and Boston, MA: Brill, 2010), p. 179.

9   'The little village that could: Shenzhen reinvents itself, set to surpass H.K.', *Bloomberg* [website] (11 May 2015). Available at https://www.bloomberg.com/news/articles/2015-05-11/the-little-village-that-could-shenzhen-set-to-surpass-hong-kong.

10 Kam Wing Chan, 'A road map for reforming China's hukou system', *chinadialogue* (22 October 2013). Available at https://www.chinadialogue.net/article/show/single/en/6432-A-road-map-for-reforming-China-s-hukou-system.

11 Tom Phillips, 'China's multimillionaires emigrating in droves', *Telegraph* (18 December 2012). Available at http://www.telegraph.co.uk/news/worldnews/asia/china/9753145/Chinas-multimillionaires-emigrating-in-droves.html.